THE REFERENCE SHELF   VOLUME 45 NUMBER 3

THE BUSINESS OF SPORTS

EDITED BY

WILLIAM P. LINEBERRY

THE H. W. WILSON COMPANY

NEW YORK   1973

THE REFERENCE SHELF

Copyright © 1973

By The H. W. Wilson Company

PRINTED IN THE UNITED STATES OF AMERICA

Library of Congress Cataloging in Publication Data

Lineberry, William P   comp.
   The business of sports.

   (The Reference shelf, v. 45, no. 3)
   Bibliography: p.
   1. Sports—Economic aspects—Addresses, essays, lectures. 2. Sports—Economic aspects—United States—Addresses, essays, lectures. I. Title. II. Series.
GV716.L56   338.4'7'7960973   73-8940
ISBN 0-8242-0506-5

PREFACE

What is the most expensive sport? the most popular? the one involving the most money? the best paying in terms of professionals' salaries? the one with the biggest television audience? the one in which salaries are rising fastest? * In this era of the sports craze in America, the answers to such questions are almost as important as the traditional ones about who leads in home runs, passes completed, baskets scored in a single game. The popular tensions generated at contract time, when players and their lawyers lock in Byzantine bargaining with owners and their financiers, are almost as taut as the closing minutes of a fiercely contested game. And who is to say that the record salary of $200,000 a year being drawn by Hank (The Hammer) Aaron of the Atlanta Braves is not as enthralling a matter to fans (and to Aaron) as the fact that he is the greatest long-ball slugger in baseball today?

Sports writers are traditionally a cynical lot, but when the name of the game increasingly sounds like "Money," perhaps a measure of cynicism is well deserved. And yet there is nothing really new or shocking in the fact that sports is a business in America—and a big business at that. For every team run strictly by the profit and loss ledger of an accountant, somewhere there is another run—often deeply in the red—by a philanthropic millionaire who either loves the sport or loves the prestige and glamour attached to the owner's box on the 50-yard line or behind first base. That money is the inevitable lubricant which keeps the wheels of this multimillion dollar industry spinning is hardly cause for shame or despair.

* According to the *Guinness Sports Record Book,* yachting is the most expensive sport; the most popular today by all accounts is pro football; horse racing involves the most money, while pro basketball pays best in terms of professionals' salaries; pro football enjoys the biggest TV audience; and it is in hockey that salaries are currently rising fastest.

And yet, again, ends and means seem to be growing confused. Is it money that makes the game possible or vice versa? Are all the old traditions of team spirit, player loyalty, and respect for the paying fan being traded for a mess of dollars? Certainly, there are owners who treat players like prize beef to be sold to the highest bidder. And certainly there are players who handle their careers as though they were major industrial enterprises instead of particular talents on the playing field. Certainly, too, the fans who pay the bills have been jarred and maybe even disillusioned by team owners who switch franchises for the sake of a greater profit or by the rapid spread of new franchises—a growth which has the effect of stretching available talent so thin that the "pro" in pro sports is drawn into question.

When all the hustling is set aside, when the commercial trappings and gimmicks are stripped away, when all the dollars have been divided, distributed, and pocketed, is there any love for the sport itself left, either on the playing field or in the stands?

If some of the articles in this compilation are an accurate measure, the answer is a gloomy one. But as other articles also make clear, sports in America today are nonetheless enjoying a vital boom. Somewhere, someone must be doing something right. The object of this volume is to cast a glance at the business aspects of sports in America now, to gauge their impact on the games people play and on society itself. As the first section in this compilation indicates, sports is obviously a big and lucrative business, though not without its financial problems. For the moment, at least, pro football seems to have captured the hearts of the country from the President on down and is enjoying a financial surge of unprecedented proportions. Pro basketball and hockey appear to be coming up fast, as well, although that "great American pastime," baseball, is suffering somewhat from the slow pace of its games and an overly long season. Perhaps the essential elegance of baseball is in danger of being squeezed out in an era that appears to prize the fast pace and rough-and-tumble of more violent spectacles. The sport that attracts more money than all the rest combined—horse racing—is certainly alive and kicking, as is that one sport which has yet to be relegated to a wholly spectator status—golf.

The second section examines some of the more blatant commercial trappings of the sports industry. Will free pantyhose help fill the stands for the Washington Senators? How can Baltimore cash in on its reputation as "city of champions," and how can auto dealers around the country make the Superbowl a cash nexus for the sale of more cars?

Sections III and IV examine the role of promoters and of players, respectively, in the chase for the dollar. If sports are being tailored for television, and if television is tailored for advertising, is the game of the week really a game at all or merely a means for selling beer? And if sports heroes make more money selling the proverbial shaving cream off the field than they do on, where do they find the time actually to work at their profession?

The fifth section indicates that for all the hustle for a buck (or perhaps because of it?) many sports, including college athletics, are facing severe financial woes. The last section is devoted to issues of reform and redemption. It may be gratifying for the reader to know that Americans still spend far more on participation sports than they do as spectators in the grandstands and that a trend toward hiking, camping, boating, and bicycling may be responsible for those growing numbers of empty seats in stadiums on weekends.

The compiler wishes to thank the authors and publishers who have courteously granted permission for the reprinting of their materials in this book. He is especially indebted to his wife, Stephanie, for her help in the preparation of the manuscript.

WILLIAM P. LINEBERRY

May 1973

CONTENTS

III. THE PROMOTERS

IV. THE PLAYERS

V. ALL THAT GLITTERS

VI. Regulation, Reform, and Redemption

I. SPORTS AS AN INVESTMENT

EDITOR'S INTRODUCTION

Muckraking has rarely been the province of the sports-writer in the past. But the articles in this section demonstrate—some passionately and some with cool objectivity—that it may be the trend in the future. The following contributions may also explain why the name of the game is increasingly spelled $ports.

Of all people, perhaps, Americans should be least shocked by the business aspects of sports—the importance of the dollar in the calculations of players and owners alike, the sheer amount of money involved. One might even suggest that, as with Joe Namath, star quarterback of the New York Jets, many Americans actually expect their hero-athletes to be as tough and demanding when it comes to money as they are when it comes to winning the game. All those extras—the swank bars trading on the hero's name, the TV commercials with their fat royalties—may add to the glamour and status only of one whose talents are especially deserving of reward, anyway. Such "cashing in" proves that our heroes are as smart as they are talented.

Sometimes, however, the atmosphere of materialism gets particularly thick. The first article in this section traces the historic relationship between money and sports in America and concludes somewhat bitterly that the profits of owners, as opposed to the desires of the fans or the players, are the driving force in the industry today. *Feudalism,* says Paul Hoch, a writer with a keen interest in the sociology of sports, is the best word for describing the system by which owners are running—and ruining—professional sports in our time.

The remaining six articles in this section are given over to a survey of the financial condition of six of our major sports today. Thanks to the inflow of TV revenues, in large part, pro football is enjoying continued good times, although not every club in both leagues is in the black. Structurally, basketball is on shakier legs, with one strong league leading an upsurge in nationwide attendance and another, weaker, league lagging behind. In some respects, however, the big money is flowing more readily in pro basketball today than it is in pro football.

Hockey is only now coming into the big time as a sport of national interest to Americans, and the fourth article in this section describes the impact that one great star—in this case, Bobby Orr of the Boston Bruins—can have on an athletic stepchild which has traditionally taken a back seat to other team games. The figures in hockey, according to freelance sports writer Tom Dowling, are also beginning to run into the millions.

In the rush of the three sports noted above to box-office stardom, baseball has, to mix a metaphor, been left somewhat at the starting gate. In fact, as the contribution included here from *Forbes* magazine makes clear, baseball has been on something of a downhill run (to mix yet another metaphor) in recent years. Such is certainly not the case with either horse racing—the nation's biggest money sport—or golf, as the last two articles in this section clearly show.

MONEY AND SPORTS: A HISTORY OF THE MARRIAGE [1]

The first professional baseball team was "owned" by the players themselves, and embodied a kind of players' control over when, where, and how they should play, as well as how profits should be shared. At the time, most other baseball

[1] From *Rip Off the Big Game: The Exploitation of Sports by the Power Elite*, by Paul Hoch, writer on the political sociology of sports. Doubleday (Anchor Books). '72. p 40-52. Copyright © 1972 by Paul Hoch. Reprinted by permission of Doubleday & Company, Inc.

players also liked the idea of this arrangement. It took more than a third of a century to convince most of them that anyone else should "own" their labor or their contracts. (The basketball players took even longer.) And even in our enlightened era, many are still not convinced.

Prior to 1876, when the National League was formed, professional baseball players often moved around between whichever teams would pay them the most money, or they formed their own teams. But the capitalists who formed the new league had other ideas. They had the money for sports fields, promotion, and players' salaries, but they insisted that players sign contracts containing what was known as a reserve clause, giving their "owners" the right to reserve their services, and exclude them from playing for other league teams. This infuriated the players, but since these owners seemed to be the only ones around able to borrow the money to bankroll such a large-scale operation (and since a good many players earned big money "fringe benefits" by fixing games) most grudgingly took their pay packets and played the game.

In 1882, however, the American Association was formed. Although the new league also had what the players called a slave system—whereby owners doled out amongst themselves monopolistic rights for contracting certain players—at least now players could choose between the two leagues. This meant owners had to compete for them. But this free competition lasted only one year. The owners of the two leagues finally decided among themselves that monopoly was best for all of them, and they agreed not to hire each other's players. So the players were right back where they started.

In 1884, just eight years after the National League was founded, its monopolistic ways of doing business were put to a stern test. Realtor Henry V. Lucas declared that the reserve rule "reserves all that is good for the owners." Since it was time to do something about the player's "bondage," he formed a new Union League. Naturally, the threat of free competition did not endear itself to the monopolists or their friends in the press. It was all-out war. But, as its finances plunged deeper and deeper into the red, the Union League collapsed after only one year. As part of the price of peace and profit, Lucas himself was admitted to the National League as owner of the St. Louis franchise. Monopoly was still intact.

Smashing the Players' League

The owners had a good thing going, until they started pushing the players too hard. As the 1880s ended they were trying to establish a sort of productivity scale for players, whereby each man would be graded on his playing from A to E, with salaries ranging in five grades from $2,500 down to $1,500. In effect, this would have taken away the player's right to negotiate his salary with the only boss he was allowed to work for. Full-scale rebellion broke out. Under the leadership of their union, the National Brotherhood of Professional Players, the athletes set up their own league. The National League was decimated. Even by paying huge salaries, it could hold so few of its players that it had to fill almost every position with rookies. It became known as the sand-lot league. The American Association found itself in a similar position. The Players' League promptly managed to attract more fans than either of the old leagues. Not surprisingly, other capitalists, including those who owned the newspapers, did not like the idea of workers deserting a business and setting up their own. So the new league found it impossible to raise money. It could not get bank loans. More often than not, its games received no press coverage. . . . Without financial backing from the banks, the players found it hard to stand up to cutthroat competition. In a year this most popular of the three leagues, comprised of almost all the top players, had folded. The American Association (which used to refer to the NL as "the rich man's league") went down shortly thereafter. The players had been beaten back. The rule of monopoly continued.

College Sports as Business

The situation in other sports had been a bit better. High school and college sports, of which football was rapidly becoming the most popular, were for many years entirely under the control of the players themselves. Intramural and even intercollegiate games were simply organized by the students interested in such things, without much interest or interference from school administrations. For example, in his book *The Athletic Revolution* Jack Scott notes that in the 1860s high school football matches between public and private schools became popular around Boston, and 1869 saw the first major American college football game, between Princeton and Rutgers. "American schools and colleges," he says, "followed the pattern of Oxford and Cambridge during the beginning years of interscholastic and intercollegiate competition, and the responsibility for organizing athletic programs remained in the hands of the undergraduates." It should be added, however, that these athletic activities developed for the most part at highly elite prep schools and universities where no one would have dreamed of ordering about and controlling the gentleman-players in the authoritarian manner that has become so common today.

In the 1880s, however, two things happened. First, college sports started spreading far beyond the elite colleges of the Ivy League and the Northeast to places, including especially the church-run schools like Notre Dame, which had no tradition of student-organized activities. More important, as the popularity of college football grew, the opportunity was seized to turn it into a big business. It was not long before the undergraduate sports programs were taken out of the hands of the undergraduates, and placed in the hands of a small elite clique of alumni, usually from the wealthiest families, who could be expected to exercise the same disproportionate influence on the college as a whole as they did on its sports program. In fact, in a very real sense the sports program *became* the college.

Frederick Rudolph, in his book *The American College and University* points out that in the 1890s at schools like Notre Dame sports became, in effect, the main agency for student recruitment. Even where this did not happen to such a great extent, college sports were to the outside world still the most visible—usually the *only* visible—part of college life, and functioned almost as a public relations program, helping to perpetuate the image of the well-rounded college man. "By 1900," says Rudolph, "the relationship between football and public relations had been firmly established and almost everywhere acknowledged as one of the sport's major justifications."

College Sports as Public Relations

This mythical connection between the college sports program and the fiction of the well-rounded college man was particularly ironic, because the college sports programs came into vogue at precisely the same time as well-roundedness was being destroyed by the increasing demands for specialization. With the possible exception of the elite Ivy League schools, the college regimen became increasingly the factory-like one of greater fragmentation of disciplines, proliferating bureaucracies, and greater specialization. Instead of "well-rounded" men, the grads began increasingly to resemble mass-produced products. "Progressive" educators decided not to attack this proliferating specialization, but instead to add into the high school and college curricula a "liberal" sample of extra-curricular frills, including athletic teams and intramural programs, student government, societies, and whatnot. Then the high schools and colleges could still produce the specialized robots required by the new mass-production monopolies and yet claim to be giving everyone a well-rounded education. It was precisely the solution that the factory owners themselves had opted for when they introduced factory sports programs to "broaden" the interests of their workers. High school and college sports were drafted to serve as the Emperor's clothes for an increasingly empty and dehumanizing style of education. They were good public relations, and brought in money, too.

Until the 1960s the money-making side of college sports was still important. College football at major schools could be depended upon to provide support for every other sport, and probably a good part of the academic program as well (either directly or through the contributions a winning team attracted from wealthy alumni). And the emphasis was mainly on winning, almost as an end in itself. However, in the sixties, in the era of expensive athletic scholarships and slush funds, multiple-platoon teams, and declining student interest, football at a great many places was no longer even self-supporting, and had to be justified, to an increasing extent, as basically a public-relations expense.

In basketball there was much more flexibility. Not only was the sport not invented until around 1891, but it was to be dominated by player-controlled teams throughout most of its history. This came to a decisive end after World War II, when owners of sports arenas in the big cities decided there was big money to be made from professional basketball. So they formed their own league (soon to become the National Basketball Association). In competing with players' teams and non-league owners' teams, their one major advantage was control of the arenas (i.e., the means of sports production). They did not have to be so heavy-handed as to exclude the other teams entirely, although this sometimes happened. All they had to do was raise the rental price of the arena to the point where almost no one could afford it. (The arena owners, of course, could afford it, since in booking their facilities for their own teams, they were paying themselves!) Thereafter, pro basketball, too, was monopolized and controlled by just a handful of "owners."

Who Controls Sports?

So throughout the sports industry, as in every other industry under capitalism, control is exercised, not by the consumers (fans), nor by the producers (players), but by the

owners of capital. It is they who decide whether or not to
stage their spectacles and when, where, and how to do so.
Ownership gives them the power to dictate the complete
development or non-development of the industry, the very
life and working conditions of those (players) whose labor
they buy, and the nature of the product they produce. And
the basis of their decisions is, first and foremost, personal
profit. In this, sports owners are just like other capitalists
(although some of them may, incidentally, be big sports fans
on the side). However their loyalty to their capital will always surpass their loyalty to the team. If it did not they
might quickly find themselves out of business. And there is
a lot of money involved.

Indeed, the first thing we notice about the sports industry is that it is very expensive to become an owner. When
the first professional baseball league was formed in 1871 the
entrance fee for a team was just ten dollars. Five years later,
when the National League was formed, the price of a franchise was just one hundred dollars plus players' salaries. By
the mid-1960s, CBS had bought the New York Yankees for
$15 million and later the Vancouver Canucks hockey team
was purchased for $6 million. At these prices a situation is
rapidly being created in which only corporations of substantial size, or syndicates of their executives, can raise the
capital to buy a team. Under these conditions, a professional
sports operation becomes little more than a cog in a giant
corporate empire (or syndicate of interlocking directorates)
and is run in the same way as the rest of the enterprise.
"There's not much need, really, to document football's place
in the great American free-enterprise system," wrote a columnist in the Toronto *Telegram's Weekend Magazine*. "All
pro sports are run as efficiently, cold-bloodedly and greedily
as any other big business with a lust for a buck." As elsewhere in the "game" of capitalist big business, we find boards
of directors dictating from the top to their production managers who dictate to supervisors (coaches) dictating to

workers (players). And the latter have been reduced to little more than pawns in a giant corporate machine concerned much more with profit than "play."

How Much Are Sports Worth?

It is instructive to gauge the size of the American sports business. Every year about 300 million admission tickets are bought for major sports events. An average take of at least $6 a head for admissions, confectionery, and parking gives an estimate of gross revenues of around $1.8 billion. Adding in revenues derived from the sale of TV rights brings the total to around $2.5 billion. In addition, a 1959 report from the First Federal Reserve Bank of Philadelphia estimated that such direct participation sports as boating, swimming, fishing, bicycling, roller skating, bowling, hunting, baseball and softball, pool, golf, tennis and skiing involved at least 286 million Americans and resulted in expenditures (mainly for equipment and travel) of over $10 billion. (The present figure is about double that.) In 1966 the United States Department of Commerce estimated the country's annual recreational expenditure (including sports and related entertainment and travel) at around $30 billion. We must also include the billions annually invested in such facilities as stadiums, practice fields, arenas, field houses, sports advertising, media equipment to cover sports events, costs of processing and distributing sports news ad infinitum. Although there is considerable overlap in these various figures, it seems apparent that total sports and sports-related expenditures in the United States cannot be less than around $25 billion annually. (And this says nothing whatever about the tens of billions made off products marketed via sports *machismo*.)

And it's not just the proceeds from the games, or the advertising, that makes sports such a lucrative enterprise. A 1963 article in the *Financial Post* noted that preparations for the Tokyo Olympics had sparked a rebuilding job costing a tidy $1.5 billion (including a $550 million rail line between Tokyo and Osaka, twenty-three new arteries and eight expressways into the city [mostly from the airport], nine miles of new subway, additions to the Tokyo police force and an $18 million television center capable of providing round-the-world coverage).

In preparation for the smaller 1968 Winter Olympics, Grenoble built a new city hall, post office, hospital, police station, school, exhibition hall, airport, railway station, cultural center, and various multilane highways. All told, it came to a $200 million investment. The *Financial Post* described it as "Grenoble's hopes of becoming a leading European city, an international convention center, a city trying to establish a reputation as France's 'City of Tomorrow' or 'Atlantic City.' . . ." (Nancy Greene, who won a skiing gold medal at Grenoble points out in her autobiography that, with this kind of money at stake, it was necessary to appeal to a gigantic audience to pay for it all: "The result inevitably is that the Olympic Games descend to the level of spectacle and begin to resemble some kind of circus.")

. . . [In 1972] the New York Yankees' bosses . . . [succeeded in persuading] the city to rebuild Yankee Stadium for them at a cost of around $30 million. [Construction had not yet begun in the spring of 1973.—Ed.] The Detroit Lions' and the Detroit Tigers' brass are reportedly dickering to have the taxpayers build them a new stadium (possibly two) at a cost variously estimated as running around $150 million. The Yankees, it will be remembered, are owned by CBS, a corporation worth billions of dollars. The Lions are owned by William Clay Ford, vice president and part owner of the Ford Motor Company, and reportedly worth around $140 million. Multimillionaire John Fetzer, who owns the Tigers, also owns the "Tiger Network" of eight radio stations as well as various television interests. And these are the sports magnates the taxpayers are supposed to be subsidizing to the tune of hundreds of millions for their stadiums!

Meanwhile the Detroit Board of Health has termed some sixty thousand of that city's houses as substandard or unfit for human habitation.

In hockey, it's been a similar story. Without a big enough arena it was implied that Vancouver could not get a National Hockey League franchise. So Canadian taxpayers were encouraged to build the $6 million Pacific Coliseum. The government in Ottawa and the British Columbia provincial treasury each put up $2 million. The city of Vancouver added $1.75 million, and the Pacific National Exhibition (which owns the Coliseum building) added the final quarter million. The Vancouver Canucks were 87 percent American-owned. So, what you had was three levels of Canadian government forking out about $6 million so that American millionaires could sell a Canadian game to Canadians.

Monopoly Ownership

One reason an aspiring sports magnate is willing to pay millions of dollars for a team is that the possession of a league franchise puts him in a monopolistic position in marketing his product in a particular city and hiring the players who will produce the product. The toleration by the dominant elements in society of such monopolistic agreements in restraint of a free-player market, as the reserve and option clauses written into all major-league contracts, reflects the usefulness of the sports industry in providing a profitable investment channel for their surplus capital, and even more importantly, for furthering the sort of competitive, work-hard, be-disciplined, produce-more, consume-more ideology our capitalists find so attractive. The laws governing sports, including especially the 1922 Supreme Court decision exempting baseball from the anti-trust laws, arise out of both the economics of this capitalist industry and the place of sports production, including ideological indoctrination, in this society generally. Thus, the sports industry provides a graphic illustration of how, when the economic situation in a major industry violates the laws of capitalist society (in this case, the anti-trust laws), the laws are re-interpreted to agree with the economic "realities" and not the other way around. ...

Tax Loopholes

Owners are allowed not only full control over markets and players, but also tremendous tax loopholes. Since they have always considered players as "property" it was only a matter of time before they started claiming the same sort of depreciation allowances as the oil industry. The way this "game" is played has been described by former Chicago White Sox owner Bill Veeck in his aptly titled book, *The Hustler's Handbook*. When buying a major-league team, says Veeck, you can imagine that you are buying their whole operation —team plus franchise—or you can claim to be buying a franchise plus a series of players. In the first case, the players would be considered an "existing asset, which the previous ownership had already written off at the time of their original purchase" and you would not be eligible for any further tax write-offs to cover further depreciation. On the other hand, if you bought "the players from the old company before you liquidated, in distinct and separate transactions," they can be listed as an expense item. "It said so right in your books." You can then depreciate the cost of each player over a period ranging from about three to ten years, which you estimate to be his useful playing life. "If you expect to make a lot of money fast, you're better off being able to write them off as quickly as possible." If not, you choose the longer period.

The key is the amount of the purchase price of the team you assign to the players, and how much you claim as the cost of the franchise. In the early sixties, it was customary in baseball to estimate the worth of the franchise (i.e., the part that cannot be depreciated) as a mere $50,000. This left the new owners free to list around 98 percent of the purchase price as an expense item—i.e., player costs—which they could then use for tax write-offs. (In fact, during base-ball's expansion in the mid-sixties, there was no charge at all for the franchises; everything was supposedly being spent for tired, old, cast-off players.)

Veeck gives the example of the sale of the Milwaukee Braves just before they moved to Atlanta. After deducting the $50,000 franchise fee, the "cost of players" came to about $6 million. Depreciation over ten years would then give the new owners an annual tax write-off of about $600,000. Or, put slightly differently, they would pay *no taxes at all* on their first $600,000 of profit (and since the corporate tax runs about 50 per cent, they would be saving themselves around $300,000 a year for ten years, or $3 million). "If you want to be cynical, you might even say the Government was paying half of their purchase price for them."

Depreciating Athletes

You might think that the owners would still have to pay taxes on any profits above $600,000. Wrong again. They can spend them on new players, and then start depreciating them. After ten years they sell, and then somebody else starts the tax-write-off game all over again. It is important to see that they are not selling just a franchise and a team: they are selling, says Veeck, *"the right to depreciate."* This is the real reason the price of a major-league team has been in-creasing steadily, since the more the price rises the larger the depreciation write-off becomes. But at these prices a situ-ation is being created in which only corporations can afford to bid. CBS and the Yankees is the obvious example, but the Montreal Expos, Los Angeles Angels, Detroit Tigers, and St. Louis Cards were all bought on behalf of substantial corporate empires (a whiskey company, various television and radio interests, and a brewery, respectively). "A cor-poration," says Veeck, "not only has the money, *but it can use the depreciation write-off on its total corporate profits even if the ball club itself hasn't made enough profit to cover it.*" He adds that, of the ten American League clubs in existence when he wrote his book, only two were not tied in some way to established profit-making corporations that could absorb either the operating losses or the player depreciation and, happily, "pass 50 per cent of the price on to the Government." No wonder Veeck says our national pastime is not baseball but "how to make sure profits can be claimed as a capital gain rather than as income."

PRO FOOTBALL STRIKES IT RICH [2]

Reprinted from *U.S. News & World Report.*

From a struggling sport to a booming, ninety-million-dollar-a-year business—That is the success story of professional football, now opening another record-breaking season.

Businessmen who invested in major-league-football franchises have seen the value of their investments double, triple —or rise even more—in just a few years.

Teams bought in the 1950s for less than a million—or in the early 1960s for 4 to 5 millions—now sell for 10 to 16 millions. Examples: The Philadelphia Eagles, Cleveland Browns and New York Jets, whose stories are told below.

Football fortunes are being made by players as well as by owners. Young men just out of college have earned hundreds of thousands of dollars in a few years playing pro football.

Gone is the era of the huge bonus, when college stars were lured to pro teams by sums such as the $600,000 guaranteed halfback Donny Anderson by the Green Bay Packers in 1966 or the $400,000 guaranteed quarterback Joe Namath by the New York Jets in 1965.

Since the National Football League (NFL) and the American Football League (AFL) agreed in 1966 to a common draft, there is no longer competitive bidding between them for football talent.

[2] From "Pro Football's Boom: From Sport to Glamour Industry." *U.S. News & World Report.* 67:82-4. S. 22, '69.

Yet O. J. Simpson, a star back from the University of Southern California, reportedly received a guarantee of $215,000 in salary—plus a $100,000 loan—in a four-year contract signed ... with the Buffalo Bills.

Players' salaries have more than doubled in a decade. Payroll figures are not made public, but authoritative estimates are that the average salary is about $25,000 a year and at least half the players make $20,000 or better. A few superstars, such as quarterback Johnny Unitas of the Baltimore Colts, are believed to earn in the neighborhood of $100,000 annually.

All this pay is for a working season that lasts less than six months.

Attendance is twice what it was . . . [in 1960]. Counting postseason playoffs, a total of 8.9 million people attended big-league games last year [1968]—11.6 million if you include preseason exhibition games and all-star games. This compares with 4.2 million attendance in 1960.

Pro football keeps expanding. It has gone from a single major league of 12 teams in 1959 to two major leagues with a total of 26 teams . . . [in 1969]. Several minor leagues also are operating.

Yet football cannot seem to expand fast enough to reach all its potential paying fans. Even with the number of games increasing—from 134 in 1960 to 182 . . . [in 1969]—the crowds at each game grow larger year by year.

In the National League, attendance at regular-season games went up from an average of 40,106 persons per game in 1960 to an average of 52,521 in 1968.

In the American League, attendance has gone up from an average of 16,538 per game in 1960—the league's first year —to 37,643 . . . [in 1969].

Countless millions of fans watch pro football on television screens. Estimates are that 60 million watched the 1969 Superbowl, in which the New York Jets beat the Baltimore Colts for the national championship, and that about 35 million watch games on a typical Sunday in midseason.

The TV Bonanza

Football's revenue from television keeps soaring.

In 1963, the two major leagues collected only $6.5 million for rights to televise their games—4.7 million going to the NFL, 1.8 million to the AFL. . . . [In 1969] TV networks are paying nearly $28 million to telecast the regular-season games alone—nearly 19 million to the NFL and 9 million to the AFL.

In addition, about $8 million will be paid for telecasts of postseason title games. This makes an over-all total of almost $36 million that pro football will get from television alone.

Sponsors pay as much as $75,000 for a single minute of advertising on a football telecast. TV revenue from regular-season games is divided equally by the 16 NFL teams, so each team is assured about $1.2 million this season [1969]. In the 10-team AFL, most teams will get nearly $1 million from TV.

All this is before selling a single ticket to a football game —and ticket sales account for almost 60 per cent of pro football's total revenue. With most tickets selling in the $5 to $6 price range—some run as high as $10—total gate receipts for the two major leagues . . . [in 1969] are expected to top $50 million.

A few additional millions will come from local telecasts, radio broadcasts, food and drink concessions, parking fees and other incidental revenue. Add it all up, and pro football will probably gross around $90 million this season [1969], compared with a gross of about 65 million in 1965.

That is a growth of 38 per cent in four years. Not many businesses grow that fast.

The financial outlook for the [1969] season now beginning is regarded as brighter than for almost any year past. Some clubs, including the Washington Redskins, already have sold every seat available for the entire season. Clubs reporting virtual sellouts include the New York Jets and the New York Giants, the Kansas City Chiefs and the Green Bay Packers.

In 1970, another gain in attendance and income is foreseen as the two major leagues complete a merger agreed upon in 1966. Although each league retains a separate identity, both operate under a central organization. . . . [In 1970] Baltimore, Cleveland and Pittsburgh will transfer from the National to the American League to create two leagues of equal size—thirteen teams in each. This is expected to prove a boost to the younger American League and result in a better economic balance between the two leagues.

Also new next year will be some Monday-night games to be telecast in addition to the usual Sunday telecasts. This will increase the total TV revenue, and likewise the income of each club.

How much more can pro football expand? How long will this boom last? Can the value of a pro-football franchise keep on soaring? Football owners themselves are beginning to wonder. Some see pro football approaching its ceilings, both in attendance and in TV markets.

Pete Rozelle, who heads both leagues as Commissioner of major professional football, told a member of the staff of *U.S. News & World Report*: "The future of pro football certainly is healthy. I wouldn't say that the boom is over. But we can hardly continue to grow at the same percentage rate as we have in the past."

In television, weekends already are crowded with football—college games on Saturday, doubleheaders in each professional league on Sunday. Monday-night telecasts are coming. How many more can be added?

The number of seats in stadiums puts a limit on the number of tickets that can be sold. . . . [In 1968] the NFL sold tickets for 88 per cent and the AFL for 75 per cent of all available seats. A few new stadiums are being built—in Philadelphia, Pittsburgh, Cincinnati and Dallas. Some others are planned. But the net result will be the addition of relatively few thousands of seats.

Unless prices are raised, there is not much room for growth from ticket sales—and most club owners express reluctance to boost prices much higher.

A Cost Squeeze

Costs of operating a team meanwhile keep rising at a rapid rate. One team says its costs have gone up 35 per cent in four years.

As in most businesses, a large part of the cost rise is in salaries. The total payroll of a typical NFL club was only about $150,000 in 1939, half a million dollars in 1961, and is about 1.4 million . . . [in 1969]. One owner reports his player payroll has tripled since 1961.

Pensions and fringe benefits for players have increased. Now a veteran of ten years in the major leagues can look forward to a pension of more than $1,100 a month at age sixty-five.

Expansion has boosted travel expenses. It costs an east coast club many thousands of dollars to go to the west coast for a game.

The price of uniform and equipment for a single player has risen above $300.

The New York Giants one year paid about half a million dollars to players who could not play because of injuries.

Every time a fan makes off with a ball kicked into the stands it costs some club about $27.

Owners generally insist that the operating profits of a club are small in comparison with the millions invested.

Official figures on profits and losses are rarely made public. But owners of the NFL, for the purpose of negotiating with the Players Association, put together a "schedule of operating income and expense averages" for the 1967 season which provides a general view of football's financial picture. According to that report:

The average revenue of each NFL club in 1967 was $3.8 million.

The average expenses of each club were $3.2 million.

Average net "operating income before amortization of player contracts and other acquisition costs, other expenses and income taxes" was $635,000.

Some AFL teams lost money regularly in their early years.

These returns are on investments valued at $10 million to $16 million.

Why, then, do some businessmen seem willing to pay these ever-rising prices to buy a ball club?

"You've really got to love the game," says Art Modell, principal owner of the Cleveland Browns.

Mr. Modell and his associates bought the Browns in 1961 for about $4 million. The team had sold for about $600,000 in 1953. Today it is estimated it would bring $14 million or more. Yet Mr. Modell told a member of the staff of *U.S. News & World Report*:

> Pro football is not a prudent business investment. It is too unpredictable. Operating profits never justify your investment. The only way to make money is to sell your club at a profit—and at a capital-gains tax rate.
>
> But there is no room in pro football for the smart businessman who is looking to turn his money over in a year or two for a quick profit. He'll get hurt. [See "Trouble for the Front Office," in Section V, below.]

Clinton W. Murchison, Jr., who owns the Dallas Cowboys, says: "You could make more money investing in government bonds. But football is more fun."

Few club owners—perhaps half a dozen—depend on football for a livelihood. Most made their money in some other field, then bought a team.

The main hope for pro football to grow in the future is seen in creation of new teams. Commissioner Rozelle speculates that eventually six clubs may be added to make two leagues of sixteen teams each—and that some of the cities brought in may lie outside the continental United States.

Such expansion, he predicts, is several years away. Pro football's boom may slow down until that expansion comes.

BASKETBALL AS BIG BUSINESS [3]

I love basketball. It is important for people to understand that because, as much as I believe in it, I have to leave it now. There is a sickness there. It is in basketball, and it is in sports in general.

This isn't an easy thing to say, and many people won't agree. Maybe they will say that I'm just an embittered and jealous man. But they will be wrong. There is disease anywhere when cheating and deceit are ignored. In sports today, they are often applauded. Integrity is disappearing. Contracts mean nothing; not between owner and player, or owner and fan. Players jump teams. Teams jump cities. And all the while the money flows as from a cornucopia.

To me it is reprehensible that a college player like Jim Chones should be encouraged to ignore his commitments to his teammates with less than half a season to go in order to sign a pro contract, just as it is wrong that Charlie Scott and Jim McDaniels, who both jumped from the ABA [American Basketball Association] to the NBA [National Basketball Association] . . . , should ignore their professional commitments. The only difference between the vagrant pros and collegians is that the pros have business contracts while the collegians do not. Universities cling tenaciously to the opinion that they are not in the same marketplace for athletic bodies, but they are. [See "Corrupting the Amateurs" in Section II, below.]

There was a time, and it was not so long ago, when things such as honor and loyalty were virtues in sport, and not objects of ridicule. It was a time when athletes drew pleasure and satisfaction from the essence of competition, not just from their paychecks. But somehow, with the introduction of big business, the concept of sports in this country has changed.

[3] From "There Is a Disease in Sports Now . . . ," by Tom Meschery, a former basketball star and coach, currently a free-lance writer. *Sports Illustrated*. 37: 56-8+. O. 2, '72. Reprinted from *Sports Illustrated*, Oct. 2, 1972 © 1972 Time, Inc.

The Big-Business Mentality

The business psyche has invaded basketball and has made the players nothing but businessmen spurred by the profit motive. In some cases players make more money with their outside financial activities than they do on the court. Their sport becomes a mere showcase to keep them before the public, like an actor's guest appearance on a television talk-show. The game no longer has its roots sunk into idealistic bedrock. It's just business: nine to five. And that's very sad, because to me sports always have been a sort of quixotic-type existence.

I have a real hang-up about big corporation spider webs. It bothers me when I see guys stepping on each other to achieve their financial goals. And now these people, wearing big boots, are in sports, manipulating them the way some people manipulate the stock market or the price of gold.

I'm going to leave all that. Maybe someday I'll be able to return. I hope so. But the way things are now, I have to get out. I've taken my wife, Joanne, and the three children and I've been accepted into the University of Iowa's Graduate Writer's Workshop. I've had a book of poetry published, some of it about basketball. I've saved a little money and I intend to write. Much of my thinking is socialistic. I just don't care about big money. I could live a life similar to the athlete in Russia, with a steady job, and I'd be provided for and I'd know my family wouldn't starve and I'd be doing the thing that I love to do: play sports. Maybe that sounds very naive, very emotional, but it's my way of life.

People in the business world can't understand me, but that is only another symptom of the problem. Money has become so much of a ceramic god to them that they think you're demented to walk away from a job that pays a good salary. I've been called a big hippie. I'm big, but I'm not going to be a hippie. I'm a product of the 1950s and I'll never be able to change. For instance, I'll never be able to alter my concept of loyalty. To me, loyalty is important; loyalty

to the team, and teamwork, means an awful lot to me. I'm
not an individualist in that sense.

I was born in Harbin, China, thirty-three years ago. My
parents were refugees from Russia who fled when the Com-
munists took over in 1917. My father was an officer in the
White Russian army and my grandfather was a member of
the senate, and my mother was from an aristocratic family.
I've learned through them and my childhood that money is
meaningless. At one time my parents were part of the upper
class in Russia. A few years later, after much of my family
ended up in Japan, we were interned in a concentration
camp for the duration of World War II. Money was of no
value. People died there, rich and poor alike.

When our family emigrated to America in 1947, we
settled in San Francisco and lived on the edge of the Fillmore
Street ghetto. We were very poor. My father was a tanner.
And finally he became a dental technician.

As a kid, I was on the fringe of being what you might
call a hood. But while my buddies were getting into trouble,
I was in a gym working out or down at a playground. I got
into a few scrapes and was put on probation, but the point
is: I loved sport and, as the cliché goes, sport saved me.

Competing for the Big Dollar

I spent eleven years in pro basketball, ten of them as an
NBA player, and last season [1971] as coach of the Carolina
Cougars of the American Basketball Association. As a player,
I was grossly underpaid by today's standards, but I never
bargained. My last year I made $35,000. The first contract
I signed was with Eddie Gottlieb, nicknamed The Mogul,
one of the founders of the National Basketball Association.
He walked into my room at a college all-star game in Kansas
City in 1961 and asked me how much I was worth. You do
that today and the kid won't answer. His agent will, and
he'll tell you his client is worth $4 million because he led his
college team in scoring, for half a year anyway. (And the

owners pay it, which has to be the greatest practical joke I've ever heard.) I was ecstatic just to be asked to play. As a first-round choice I commanded a nice contract: $12,000 a year and a $2,000 bonus. That's not even the minimum now.

It was around 1967 or 1968 that I first began to notice the change in pro basketball. With the emergence of the ABA, the competition for the big dollars started, and the old owners no longer fitted in. They were basketball men, pure and simple. Certainly they bargained over nickels and dimes, but it was understandable. They didn't have a lot of money to work with. Men like Eddie Gottlieb of the Warriors, Ben Kerner of the St. Louis Hawks and Danny Biasone of Syracuse stood in the lobbies selling the tickets, rushed to their offices to count the money, then headed for the dressing rooms to pay the players' salaries. The players' demands for big money finally forced these men out, and brought in new owners who were concerned with sports only in a business sense. Now the bed is made and they're in it, players and owners together, side by side.

The players have no rapport with the owners. They know that they are simply their bosses' ego objects. The owners think: "I own Wilt Chamberlain. I own Kareem Abdul-Jabbar. I own. I possess. I can go to a cocktail party and talk about how these are my guys." But to Eddie and Danny and some of the others, it was different. When my father died, I was in the army and I needed money to pay his bills. I called Eddie Gottlieb. The money was on the way that day. And he never took it out of my salary. It paid my dad's hospital bills.

Today's owners have no real commitment to sport. Now instead of paying a player for the job he can do for the team, the owners pay him for his publicity and public-relations value. Look what Madison Avenue has done with Pete Maravich: his hair goes to the right, his hair goes to the left, his hair goes in for a lay-up. He is one of the few young players whose huge contract the owners do not complain

about. After all, they tell you, Pete has already attracted
enough extra fans in Atlanta to more than pay his tab. What
they do not tell you is that Maravich is only a good, improving ballplayer. He might eventually become a great one, but
he was certainly not worth a $1.8 million contract, particu-
larly when the disgruntlement Pete's high salary caused
among the Hawks' established players is taken into account.
And if the fans go out to see an athlete put the ball behind
his back when a chest pass would get the job done, then
they're just as silly as the owners who pay the $1.8 million.

Double-Crossing Agents

Agents are another symptom of the fever that pro basketball is running. Many of them are the products of deceit,
and its master. Talk about double crossers! How about an
agent who makes a deal with a club to deliver one of his
players at a lower price if the club will pay another of his
players a higher salary? It happens. How about an agent
who takes a kickback from a club in return for delivering
his client at a lower figure? It happens. Agents pay off college
coaches, then negotiate for the coach's seniors—after they
have been properly introduced, through the coach, of course.
They lend college kids money or give them clothes, even
automobiles, in return for an exclusive right to negotiate
their contracts—then they charge 15 percent, at least, for
their services. They talk kids into giving them power of attorney. The list of abuses and behind-the-back dealing goes
on and on. One of the worst problems is that some agents
rip their percentage right off the top of the young players'
huge salaries and bonuses. Then they disappear without
ever attempting to provide their clients with even the sim-
plest sort of assistance, such as hiring lawyers to oversee the
execution of those extremely complex contracts the agents
were responsible for drafting in the first place.

What fans do not realize is that ultimately they are the
ones who pay those inflated salaries. It is all passed down

from the big people in sports and television to the little people. The consumer, a/k/a the fan, just pays a little higher price in the stores, that's all. It's getting so people can't afford sports in America. There was a time when sports provided cheap entertainment for ordinary folks. Now they are becoming a plaything of the rich.

Meanwhile, with all of this emphasis on money, we are turning out dehumanized athletes, conditioning them early to strive only for those talents that ultimately will make them rich. It starts in the Little Leagues and the Pee Wee Leagues. By the time a boy reaches high school, he is all "sloganed-out." He has been programmed to believe winning is every-thing. But winning is far from everything. If it were, losing would be nothing. And if losing is nothing, then sports should not exist.

Young players today spend all their time learning skills when they should be enjoying competition. We stress the learning process at the expense of absorbing simple, genuine enthusiasm. Pre-high-school sports should be directed toward spontaneity, not organization. They should be directed toward lessening tension, not creating it. There is no need for high school state basketball tournaments. This may seem drastic, but at that age it seems counterproductive to arrive at an ultimate winner when we could have half a dozen winners. It is good for the young to argue the never-to-be-settled championship. And if we did away with the pressures and stresses on achieving fame and greatness at a young age, we also would do away with the professional ambitions that weigh so heavily on many of today's high school coaches.

High school coaches emphasize championships and win-ning, but there is a noticeable decrease in the enthusiasm of high school boys toward sports. They don't reject sports in the way people think of dropouts, but in the casual way of the young. If there is a parallel to the games of the 1970s, it can be found in the war games played by many of the sons of medieval noblemen, or the games played by the Indian children years ago. They were taught to play at war, to refine skills that would help them become formidable warriors. It appears that we have substituted sports games for war games. Our children must be physically fit—not to have fun, but to achieve excellence. To make mistakes while competing is, sadly, no longer a joking matter.

Just Another Job

Dave Meggyesy compared football to war. In a sense you could say that about all sports today. They are as serious as war. But the difference between Meggyesy and myself is that I am not embittered about the game of basketball. It is the most beautiful game there is because it is the only team sport in which individual talents can express themselves in so many different ways. It is very much a ballet, and most of the current players are exquisite dancers. In fact, their technical skills may be overhoned. They put tremendous pride in their individual proficiencies, but some of them have little proclivity for the team game. One of the toughest problems coaches face today is whether they are going to have team basketball or be stuck with two or three players who dominate the game to the exclusion of their teammates. Many players are simply not concerned about the team concept, be it in regard to their style of play or the commitment to their teammates. Most players compete today without exuberance, without even simple enthusiasm. To them, it is just a job, one they perform without any emotional involvement.

The pro basketball fan also has changed. He is more critical now. He experiences a real letdown over a loss. It is almost as if his country has failed in war. There's no reason why a fan should leave a ball game burned out, but fans have forgotten the essence of sports: that these are games to be enjoyed.

When I announced I was quitting as coach of the Cougars . . . many people believed that the management had asked me to leave. That is wrong. I probably would have been hired by the Cougars again. But I reject the whole idea of basketball as it now exists, just as I could not allow myself to continue in something I did not believe in when I retired as a player. I could have hung on for another three or four years as a player, but that notion was very repulsive to me.

The Jim McDaniels situation influenced my decision to quit, but it was not the deciding factor. When Jim jumped the Carolina club late in the season and ultimately signed with Seattle of the NBA, I was shocked. I don't care whether he had some gripes with management. What bothers me is that there were twenty-three games to go and we were fighting for a playoff spot and he left the team. That is unbelievable. I couldn't understand it. But then again Jim probably cannot understand me saying this. He is a product of what I have been talking about. The owners went to him while he was in college and threw $1.5 million in his face and he grabbed at it. They put a beautiful snow job on him and he bought it. There was no loyalty involved, only money.

Dealing Behind Closed Doors

The funny thing is that Seattle was willing to deal Jim back to us. They wanted out. I think they saw that Jim wasn't going to turn their team around. All that proves is that the Seattle owner, Sam Schulman, has no feelings for Jim McDaniels. He doesn't care about him as a person, only as a seven-foot guy who can put a basketball through a hoop. He's his trained seal. Can you imagine Jim having to go back to Carolina where the people now despise him? He would have a nervous breakdown.

Another trouble with pro basketball is that no one wants to admit anything is wrong with it. It is a sport run behind closed doors. When I was playing and coaching, both commissioners were nothing more than cover-up men for the owners. I will be interested to see if Bob Carlson, the new

ABA commissioner, has the personal strength or the license from the owners to operate as his own man.

Certainly, in the past, league management was laughable. The area of drugs provides a good example. Everybody in the game knew for years that players were popping bennies, but no one in authority said anything until athletes started writing books about the situation. Then, suddenly, the commissioners said they were studying the problem. The funny thing is that by that time the usage of drugs had dropped considerably. In the early days of the NBA, when you had to play five games in five days—hustling on trains and small planes—you needed bennies to pep you up. But the travel situation is so much better now that you don't need the stimulants. With Carolina, if the players took pills, I never saw them do it and I wouldn't have tried to stop them if I had.

The owners are proving they are incapable of running the game. By raiding the colleges, by raiding each other's teams, by shifting their franchises, by failing to share gate receipts with their weaker members, by continually expanding only to acquire more money to meet the cost of fighting among themselves—by doing all of this, the owners are showing they cannot govern their sport. The only alternative is an impartial board, or a national sports commission, to run professional athletics.

It is possible that basketball never again can have the ideals it once did—or perhaps the cynics are right and it never had ideals and I just dreamed it did. I'm not certain. Of this I am certain: there is a disease in sports now. Especially basketball. Basketball is going to have to change, and I think it can. Just as it evolved to the stage it is now, I think it can go back to the basics again. I hope I'll be around to see it. In the meantime, I'm looking forward to going to Iowa and walking into a gym and picking up a basketball and using it just for fun again.

HOCKEY HITS THE BIG TIME [4]

The Boston Garden, home of the Celtics and the Bruins, is an ugly, massive building with the appearance of an abandoned dockside warehouse in some tough seaport town where the sun never shines. Hamburger wrappers, Dixie-cup lids, and other pieces of wind-borne trash wheel across the nearly deserted sidewalk. Ghostly, metallic squeals and clanks from subway cars stopping and starting issue from the adjacent overhead tracks. This is a dingy neighborhood by day, and at nightfall a sinister one as well.

The new Cadillac pulls into an empty parking lot, and the driver, a young man in an unassertively mod tweed suit and a long, for the moment mournful, plowboy's face, locks up his car and strides off rapidly, his shoulders hunched forward. Up ahead is another warehouselike structure with grimy window slits. The young man climbs up a truck ramp to a corrugated metal door and pushes a huge doorbell the size of a quarter. No sound echoes within, and he presses the buzzer again with urgency. More silence.

"Come on down, Bobby. Gimme an autograph," a voice calls up from the group that is gathered below.

At length the door is thrown open by a grinning janitor, who explains that the buzzer is temporarily out of order. The crowd slips off amiably into the shadows, secure in the knowledge that whoever goes in must finally come out—if he wants to redeem his Cadillac, that is.

And so Bobby Orr—defenseman for the World Champion Bruins and probably the greatest hockey player ever—makes his customary furtive entry into Boston Garden better than two hours before game time against the Minnesota North Stars. At twenty-three, stealth has become a way of life for Orr, a quiet, unassuming small-town boy from Parry Sound, Ontario. J. Edgar Hoover would have trouble prying his telephone number out of the Bruins organization. His con-

[4] From "The Orr Effect," by Tom Dowling, a free-lance sportswriter, author of *Coach: A Season With Lombardi. Atlantic.* 227:62-8. Ap. '71. Copyright © 1971, by Tom Dowling. Reprinted by permission.

tacts with the outside world are scrupulously screened by his Toronto lawyer-*cum*-business manager, Alan Eagleson.

Down in the Bruins dressing room there is another Bobby Orr on display; cavorting about in his long johns, the face, with its spadelike jaw, now beaming as he exchanges the usual locker-room salacious banter. Though his witticisms and sophistries are preserved and embellished by writers and fans alike, the truth is that they aren't very funny or profound. There is no reason, of course, why a great athlete should be a raconteur or a philosopher. Perhaps the best thing about Orr is that he has remained his own man—high-spirited, reticent—in spite of the adulation and pressure that summon him to a career as a full-blown public man and, more than that, as a catalyst for changing the structure of professional hockey.

Orr's Boston "home" is a hideout that shifts location from one hockey season to the next. This year he has sublet an apartment in a posh downtown Boston high-rise that boasts the kind of impenetrable security arrangements that would make it a natural east coast *pied-à-terre* for Howard Hughes. Recently, after many false starts leading to bolted doors, a caller (cleared by the intercession of Eagleson) located the desk clerk in the building's subterranean lobby.

"May I help you, sir?"

"Yes, I have an appointment with Bobby Orr."

The clerk cast an anxious glance at a matronly woman standing near the desk. He took the caller aside and said, "Next time you come don't mention any names. Just give the apartment number. We'll take it from there. You never can tell. We wouldn't want Bobby's apartment number to fall into the wrong hands." He stared at the matron and gave a significant nod, indicating the possibility of her leading an unauthorized autograph raid of senior citizens on Orr's secret hideaway upstairs.

And perhaps all this wariness and secrecy is warranted. For the Boston hockey fans are a raucous, possessive mobocracy with no inhibitions. . . . When the Bruins won the Stanley Cup, the Beantown honored the conquering heroes with a downtown parade, the team of twenty-odd Canadians perched uncomfortably on the back seats of convertibles.

"I always thought the only hockey fans in Boston were the same 14,994 fanatics you see every game at the Garden," Boston sports attorney Bob Woolf recalls. "My God, there were 200,000 of them lining Washington Street, just as rabid as the people in the Garden."

A Working-Class Game

The game of hockey is indeed conducted in an atmosphere of animalistic fervor—on the rink and in the stands. Earlier this season, Bruin Derek Sanderson, with his shaggy head of hair and swashbuckler's mustache covering his pinched, street urchin's face, slugged it out with enemy fans in the seats behind him while killing some time in the penalty box. For professional hockey is fundamentally a sport of the people, a working-class game played by tough brawlers and witnessed by fans just as tough and pugnacious. The hockey fans are what Sanderson calls "the lunch-bucket crowd, guys who slug their guts out all week long and whose only enjoyment is a few beers and a hockey game."

With tickets at Boston Garden selling for as high as $8, the working man expects more for his money than an effete display of Peggy Fleming ice-skating grace. He is looking for action, and hockey, a street-fighting game with no pretense at being staged for moral uplift, provides savage action aplenty, with its flailing wooden sticks, blind-side body checks on the boards, and zooming 120-mile-an-hour pucks in the air.

There is no reverence for managerial leadership here, no mirroring of middle-class aspiration, no hungering for upward mobility. Before the game, the PA system does not trumpet the hockey players' college pedigrees, since, as it turns out, many of them have no more than a ninth-grade education. The game is a calling whose apprenticeship begins as early in life as is legally possible, as in the trades pursued by the "lunch-bucket crowd." To make the whole relationship even more apposite, for years hockey players earned little more than their fans. The piddling wages, the seedy surroundings at home, the life of enforced parsimony on the road, the physical battering gave hockey a certain air of oppression. Working conditions on the rink resembled life in the sweatshop.

It should come as no surprise, then, that the ethic of hockey, like the ethic of the early labor union, is solidarity and revenge. "We got eighteen players and each'll fight for the other seventeen," says Sanderson, "and if someone gets taken out and can't get the bastard that did him in, then someone else'll pick up the banner. Sooner or later we'll get him." The fans also hunger to see vengeance enforced, and the stomping, the high-speed courtship of danger and injury indicate a strong code of group loyalty.

Owners of Wealth and Standing

Oddly enough, presiding over this down-to-earth enterprise were a small band of plutocrats, the owners of the "old six" teams—the Bruins, the Montreal Canadiens, the Toronto Maple Leafs, the New York Rangers, the Chicago Black Hawks, and the Detroit Red Wings. Unlike the founding fathers of professional football, the first hockey owners were men of wealth and social standing. The Adamses with their grocery fortune, the Norrises with their railroad and food grain millions, were amply endowed long before their entry into hockey. They were enthusiastic and dedicated sportsmen, the game having its prep school and college strand as well as its stronger working-class one. The six teams were manned by a little more than one hundred Canadian athletes drawn from a whole nation of players, thereby guaranteeing an exceptionally high level of play and an unusually clublike atmosphere of control at the top. The players were acquired and maintained like a string of racehorses. They had no choice about their future and no leverage for increasing their material wants.

Attempts to band together in a unionlike association were ruthlessly squashed, the ringleaders traded off to other teams as an example to those who might desire to upset the status quo. Hockey was a sport of serfs played to the specifications of feudal autocrats. It is no accident that one quarter of the 175 members of the Hockey Hall of Fame are "builders"—a euphemism for management—a hefty percentage of nonplaying personnel that indicates the degree to which the owners and their associates have dominated the crusty nongrowth of the sport.

Until the mid-1960s hockey remained a backwash of change, the ordinary players settling for small annual salary hikes, the superstars rewarded with more trophies than cash. Then in 1966, Bobby Orr, the All-American boy from Canada, skated into the static, confined medieval world of hockey. From the outset he was an incredibly fast and mobile skater, an instinctive playmaker, a superb stickhandler and shooter, a defenseman whose greatest skills were offensive. And this anomaly is the key to the current pre-eminence of Orr and the Bruins. Bobby's instinct is to score, to attack. He thinks not like a defenseman but like a wingman. Either by miraculous neglect or unusual foresight, his coaches have allowed him, *sui generis,* to retain his instincts in a position for which they are classically ill suited. That has made all the difference. The Bruins offense is built around Orr's keen instinct to attack; his presence on the ice makes the Boston power play irresistible. Traditional hockey defenses were not designed to cope with an attacking defenseman, thereby forcing Bruins opponents to engineer new anti-Orr defense alignments. But Orr's gifts, his speed and shiftiness, are all the more effective over the whole length of the hockey rink. The truth seems to be that he is better on offense than the NHL [National Hockey League] players assigned to cover him are on defense, a realization that has led many teams to double-cover him this year. This smothering tactic might have more merit if Orr were playing on a thinly staffed expansion team instead of the deeply talent-loaded Bruins.

How Orr Got Hooked

The upshot is that Orr's athletic abilities have permitted him to break the rules, and by breaking them successfully, he has forced a change in the offensive strategy of hockey that is potentially as revolutionary as the development of the forward pass in football. At twenty-three, he is the only athlete in North America to dominate a team sport, a total player whose presence in the lineup makes an overwhelming difference in the game's outcome.

"In my thirty-five years in the National Hockey League," says Bruins general manager Milt Schmidt, "Bobby is the greatest player I have ever seen in the past, the greatest player at present, and if anything greater than he should ever show up, I just hope the Good Lord has me around here to see him and let him be a Bruin."

"Ever since I joined this club in 1962 Orr was our Moses," says veteran Bruins goalie Ed Johnston. During the early and middle 1960s, when the Bruins were the doormat of the National Hockey League, the Boston faithful were urged to remain of stout heart until Orr turned eighteen and could legally arrive to lead the team out of the League cellar and into the playoffs.

A party of Bruins scouts had stumbled across Orr in the frozen bulrushes of Ontario back in 1960 when he was a five-feet-two-inches, 110-pound peewee, playing in an All-Ontario Bantam tournament. They began romancing Orr's parents and buttering up Parry Sound public opinion by selflessly donating $1000 a year to support kid hockey in the area. Two years later the courtship paid off, and the Bruins signed the fourteen-year-old Orr to a Junior Amateur contract that bound him to the parent club with the finality of feudal serfdom.

The cost of this transaction, like all NHL financial maneuvering, is shrouded in the deepest secrecy, but seems to have involved a new coat of stucco for the Orr's home, a secondhand car, a few hundred dollars in spare cash, and the casual promise of a new wardrobe for the indentured savior of Boston hockey. The Bruins are said to have suffered a lapse of memory on the clothing front, a misstep that was to alert the Orrs to the wisdom of getting legal counsel in future negotiations.

At fourteen Orr was assigned by the Bruins to their Oshawa Junior Amateur farm team, where, commuting almost three hundred miles round trip from his hometown to compete against players five and six years older, he made the league second all-star team in his rookie season. The publicity mills began to grind out the copy, and year by year in the Canadian amateurs Orr got better and better. Boston gloatingly passed the word to the hometown loyalists that Moses would be on hand shortly, just as soon as he became old enough to acquire a work permit. At eighteen Orr's father announced that his son was prepared to turn professional and would be represented in the contract talks by Alan Eagleson, a thirtyish Toronto lawyer who had earlier crossed swords with the NHL by representing several Maple Leaf players in disputes with Toronto management.

The Bruins were appalled. They stalled throughout the summer of 1966, testing the Orrs' resolve, blustering over their antipathy to lawyers, and in the end acknowledging that they had hoisted themselves on the petard of their own publicity campaign touting Bobby's arrival.

Eagleson is a square-jawed, hard-eyed man, a former Conservative MP [Member of Parliament] not given to wasted motion. He charges $100 an hour, so he has to produce brisk results if his clients are to afford him.

The summer-long cat-and-mouse game with the Bruins
back in 1966 could not have pleased him.

Hap Emms, the Bruins general manager at the time, kept
saying he wasn't going to meet with any lawyer [Eagleson says].
Well, hell, we had them. The Bruins had been selling Bobby like
anything back in Boston. We had the threat of letting Bobby finish
his schooling and play for the Canadian National team if they
didn't come up with a good contract. The long and short of it
was we signed a two-year contract that was the highest any rookie
had ever received up to that time, both in bonus and in salary.
The highest until then was $7000 and $7500 on a two-year basis
with $3000 to sign. We were able to get a two-year deal that was
between $50,000 and $100,000 with a $25,000 signing bonus. Now
Bobby was able to command that kind of money the year before
expansion. If he had got that kind of money when there were
twelve teams around instead of six, it wouldn't have been such a
coup, not nearly as revolutionary. With expansion there was money around. The new teams paid $100,000 to draft from the rosters
of the original six, and they had to follow up their investment by
signing the guys they drafted. Expansion doubled the number of
jobs to 240. I represented 180 of those players, by default as much
as anything, since there was no legal competition in the field. I
had eighteen of twenty Bruins. Nineteen of twenty on Pittsburgh.
What happened was that a player like Bobby Baun, who wasn't
even protected by Toronto, went from twenty thou a year to thirty
when he was drafted by Oakland. You had rookies going from
twelve thou to twenty, which was what Baun was making the year
before after ten years or so in the League. It was the old philosophy
of supply and demand.

Forming the Players Association

Orr opened the door, and expansion allowed a lot of
lesser lights to come in and join him at the hearth of prosperity. But in between these two seminal economic events
came a third, the forming of the NHL Players Association.
Having seen what Eagleson could do for Orr, the Bruins
team in December 1966, asked him to help them form the
Association.

The hockey owners among the original six make the Bruins
look liberal by comparison [Eagleson says]. The Bruins are par-
simonious, but at least they can grasp a liberal idea. Bobby's contracts, the Association and expansion forced management to re-

consider their assumptions. Owners *always* considered hockey a business, and the players *often* considered it a game. Now everyone understands that hockey is a business. In 1957 the players tried to form an association which the owners broke by trading the organizers, like Ted Lindsay, to other teams.

But the Eagleson-Orr experience demonstrated that management could be bucked and beaten. "The players were frightened of getting traded if they joined the Association at first," says Orr. "Eagleson set it up out of his own law firm. He paid to get the goddamn thing rolling."

Today the Players Association pays Eagleson $20,000 a year, which he says represents one sixth of his hockey billings and takes up half his time. He charges Orr about $25,000 a year for what he says represents one quarter of his total time. One month of the year—or 8 percent as he likes to figure it— is devoted to negotiating contracts for his other hockey clients, who collectively total about half his billings. It also means that on an hourly basis, Eagleson's regular clients are subsidizing his work for Orr and the Association. Few of them would complain of that, since without the Eagleson-Orr combine, hockey players would probably still be bumbling along negotiating their own contracts with hockey's general managers, most of whom are former players who speak fondly of the good old days.

> If you argued about money when I first came up nine years ago [says Bruins right wing John McKenzie], they . . . sent you down to the minors. Bobby wasn't scared of management, and that revolutionized the whole game. We figured if he can do it, why not us. Hell, I got a ten-to-eleven-thousand-dollar raise the year after Bobby signed.

Phil Esposito, the Bruins Plasticman contortionist on skates, who holds the NHL scoring record with 126 points in a season, sees the Orr factor, expansion, and the Association as a three-headed beast unleashed on management.

> Orr showed a good player could make good money for once. Expansion meant more teams and a demand for good players. When I first came up, you had to play ball or they'd bury you in

the minors. . . . The Association gives kids security so they can't be shipped down, since a player on the protected list has gotta be waived through the League, and it only costs $30,000 for another club to pick him off.

Yet the Association's gains in sheer dollar terms are not exactly staggering. With virtually the whole League now enrolled, in three years the Association has helped its members win a $3300 to $4000 average salary increase, plus an additional $1000 to $1500 hike in fringe benefits. The big money has still not filtered down to the ranks, though even here the Orr factor is at work.

Having signed his professional contract aboard Hap Emms's yacht back in 1966 (in a characteristic act of pique Emms refused to pose for photographers with the smiling Eagleson), Orr joined the Bruins and won the Calder Memorial trophy as rookie of the year, as well as making the second team all-star squad. The next season, though hampered by a knee injury, he won the Norris Trophy as the outstanding defenseman in the league. Meanwhile, after eight barren years the Bruins inched up into the playoffs, and Orr's contract expired.

The new pact, reported in a Toronto paper at $400,000 for three years, sent waves of consternation and paranoia through the League. The Bruins even held a press conference to denounce the figure. Most sources agree that Orr's three-year contract was in the vicinity of $200,000. "Let's just say it made Bobby at twenty the highest-paid or the second-highest-paid player in hockey," Eagleson says with a lewd grin, as if skirting away from a subject of titillating impropriety. "And Bobby was worth it. He changed the attendance around the League."

Upping the Take-Home Pay

In any case, what Eagleson sought in his new Orr contract was not cash, but tax relief—a sort of second-stage inroad on the drive for the ultimate coup, equity in the company.

I'm a firm believer in take-home pay [Eagleson says]. Taxes in Canada are much heavier than in the States. On forty thou in Canada, Bobby would have to pay thirteen, here about nine. So in his second contract we were looking for deferred payments, a public relations employment contract with the team, and certain other nonhockey concessions from the club. We put those things, along with all his promotions and endorsements, into a separate company, Bobby Orr Enterprises, which is not considered a personal corporation and which only has a 23 percent tax figure up until the first $35,000. One way or another we got Bobby's take-home pay considerably bigger than it would have been if he was just getting a salary.

Still, it was that putative $400,000 that stuck most vividly in the minds of Orr's colleagues. Eddie Westfall waggishly announced that he was half as good as Orr and accordingly deserved half as much money. Other players figured themselves two fifths as good, two thirds as good. And, of course, there were the select few, like Chicago's Bobby Hull and Detroit's Gordie Howe, who calculated present and past services and figured they were at least as good as Orr and perhaps a third better. Hull went into a protracted pout and announced his retirement from hockey before the 1968-1969 season. The Chicago Black Hawks were forced to cough up an estimated $100,000 a year to sign him. The Detroit Red Wings' Gordie Howe, who entered the NHL when pro football's "aged wonder," George Blanda, was a freshman in college, was halfway through a two-year contract when the Orr deal was announced and had to wait a year to wring an estimated $80,000 pact from Detroit. Teddy Green, the Bruins other all-star defenseman, was also working on a two-year contract when the Orr signing came, and when the Bruins refused to renegotiate, Green walked out of training camp. Both Eagleson and the Bruins tried to explain the nature of a contract, but in vain. Green sat tight.

Enter another sports attorney, Bob Woolf of Boston. At the time of the Green walkout, Woolf already had a sizable stable of football, basketball, and baseball clients.

Derek Sanderson and a few other Bruins came into the office and said, "We miss Teddy" [Woolf says]. I went to see the Bruins, and in three or four days ironed out all the differences. Teddy was misinformed. He had heard that the Bruins had renegotiated other contracts before they terminated. But the Bruins were able to show me they hadn't. I advised Teddy to rejoin the team, and that the following year when his contract expired, he would have every right to fight for a really good deal. He did, and I got Teddy a three-year contract that included a clause that if he was injured he was to get the entire amount of the contract, plus a fourth year's salary at the third year's rate.

It was to prove a providential clause, since shortly after signing the contract Green was clubbed on the head and almost died, and when he didn't was presumed destined to go through life as an invalid. This year [1971], to the astonishment of his doctors, Green is back with the Bruins.

"Yeah, Man, It's Changing"

Woolf's pride and joy, the centerpiece in his hockey collection, is Derek Sanderson, hockey's own gift to the alienated-youth market. If Orr opened up the cork of hockey's new age, Sanderson is the irksome genie the Bruins always suspected at the bottom of the bottle. "Derek's hobby is pulling everyone's chain," says Bruins president Weston Adams, Jr. "Most athletes like to be on the sports pages; Derek likes to be in the gossip columns," Bruins coach Tom Johnson notes.

"Orr is the best player in hockey," Woolf says; "Sanderson gets just as much ink on color alone. More ink. He only scored eighteen goals last year, but the average American thinks Derek's a superstar. And that puts him in line for the money on the outside."

Woolf's prize Bruin sits upstairs at the Bachelors III (the club in which he has invested on Boston's Boylston Street), spinning implausible daydreams, manufacturing

newsworthy exaggerations as is his wont. "I signed for
$55,000 this year. Base pay. I got it because, number one, the
Bruins knew I had the talent for it, and number two, they
knew I was flaky enough to quit if I didn't get it. . . ."

A caller can grasp the Bruins' reluctance to send Sanderson sallying forth on the national TV talk shows. His mono-
logues are a trifle on the bawdy side, his discussion of his
hockey salary, if frank, is overstated. Moreover, Sanderson
is the most artful of men. In spite of their rambling, not
infrequently scatological nature, his anecdotes are carefully
practiced and honed for maximum impact. For Sanderson
is interested in bringing hockey into the mainstream of
American life, with all the wealth, celebrity, and crass vul-
garity that the phrase implies. The Bruins management—
in many ways to their credit—cherishes the game's traditional
values, the independence from corporate life and TV dom-
ination, even the savagery of the game, which, unless diluted,
is too raw to gain even middle-class respectability.

Orr was hockey's inadvertent revolutionary, who changed
the economic structure of hockey by the mere existence of
his unarguable talent. Sanderson actively seeks to revolutionize the game from salaries on down.

I only had one blue suit when I came into the NHL [he says,
staring down at his embroidered shirt and bell-bottoms]. I see the
players come in the dressing room in three-button suits, dark
grays, pointed black shoes, and thin black ties. Man, they were
like machines marching in. The regimentation was terrible. I
said to myself, it's got to change. I kept the blue suit all my rookie
year. Then I won the rookie-of-the-year award, so I had some weight
behind me, and I decided to grow my hair long and I got into
mod suits and bell-bottoms. The Bruins got uptight, but after a
while they started to change too. And now all of the guys dress
sharp. I called Campbell [the NHL Commissioner] a stuffed shirt
because he wouldn't let me wear white skates, and they damn
near died. Now ther're four teams with different colored skates.
They said to me, you're too young to drive a Cadillac. Now ther're
four guys on the team with Cadillacs. They let me get away with
a little bit more every year. This year I don't wear ties to games.
That's never been allowed before in the history of the game.

Yeah, man, it's changing, but it's got to change more. The guys have got to work at it to put this game on the map.

I'd have to say management would be freer if they had more money coming in [Sanderson continues]. If you compare the gross income of management with what the players are getting, I guess it's pretty fair now. The TV has got to take off to get the big money. And the rotten truth is the game's too fast for TV. Too creative, too ad-lib, too unpredictable. The way it is now the cameras can't cover it. They have to get in too tight to follow the puck, so they miss the punches, the elbowing, hooking, tripping. You got to see those things. That's what the sport's all about.

Lagging in the Ratings War

Now that expansion has broadened hockey's base by putting franchises in eleven American cities, television remains the key to future prosperity. The new franchises gave hockey the illusion, at least, of a national market. But CBS's NHL Game of the Week has failed to capture America's Sunday afternoon sports fan deep in his rec-room armchair. National Nielsen ratings have gone from 4.1 for the 1967-1968 season to 4.8 in 1968-1969, to 5.6 for the 1969-1970 season. The network has lost money on the operation and got hockey to agree to a smaller package for the current season, which is believed to net each of the fourteen teams around $75,000 a year. The breakdown of the Nielsen ratings on a city basis tells the story: 3.8 in Atlanta, 4 in Cincinnati, 2 in Los Angeles, 3.4 in San Francisco, but 25.2 in Boston and 16.1 in neighboring Providence. Simply put, the problem is that outside New England and a few scattered Nordic pockets on the Canadian border, few Americans have played the game or are likely to in the near future. And the larger American public has never been known to pay homage to a game at which it does not excel.

As a result the new franchises in Oakland, Pittsburgh, and Los Angeles are in dire-to-disastrous financial straits, their losses hardly pared by their meager local and national TV revenues. The original six teams remain bastions of security in a shaky, somewhat uncertain hockey empire.

And the Bruins are an especially prosperous satrapy, with an annual profit believed to be between $1.75 million and $2 million. This year alone they will earn $1 million in franchise payments as their share from the entry of Buffalo and Vancouver into the League, $375,000 from their own local television contract with a UHF station that had a 42 percent regular-season rating for Bruins telecasts and a 56 percent rating for the Stanley Cup Playoffs, and an extra $600,000 from ticket sales.

We're very New Englandish [says Weston Adams, Jr.]. A debt is a matter of honor, a penny saved is a penny earned. "Cheap" is the tag line that has always gone with this organization. If running an operation conservatively, for the love of the game, is cheap, then so be it. People say, "How can you play in a dump like the Garden?" Well, it has tradition, it's one of the monuments to American hockey. Besides, it would be contrary to the way we do business to float a $15 million loan for a new hockey rink.

On the aggregate salary front we're close to the top of the League, but I'd be very surprised if we were at the top. We pay about $45,000 for our top four, but they're only twenty-five. Still, I don't think we'll ever challenge football, because hockey just isn't a very good TV game. The puck is so small, and you can't get in tight on it without losing too much of the game. And hockey doesn't lend itself to the isolated camera the way football does. I hope hockey doesn't go big on TV. TV runs football, and I don't want that. I dislike the prostituting of the game that big TV would mean. The new teams want that TV money, the older owners don't. I can't say that expansion has been a blessing for us. The other clubs are stocked with kids from our farm system. It's not cheap to fly out to Vancouver, Los Angeles, and Oakland to play. Still, you had to have expansion to prevent the kind of interleague war that football and basketball fought. Just the same, we've remained in a pretty solvent position.

Solvent enough to withstand Eagleson's impending assault to renew Orr's contract, which expires this year. From Eagleson's standpoint the tragedy is that it didn't expire last year when Orr figured so prominently in bringing the Stanley Cup to Boston for the first time in twenty-nine years. In the process he scored 120 points—only the fourth time in NHL history that any player, much less a defenseman, has gone over the 100 mark—was once again unanimously elected to the All-Star team, won four of hockey's eight major individual trophies (the other four being reserved for rookies, goalies, old-timers, and good sports), and to top things off, slammed in the winning goal to clinch the Stanley Cup in the finals against the St. Louis Blues.

What Is Bobby Worth?

Eagleson is buoyant over the future.

Look, Orr is a once-in-a-lifetime player, and the Bruins are prosperous. I find the Bruins reasonable people to deal with. They say, "Look, this is what we made last year, and this is our budget for next year, and it includes $500,000 for player salaries, so if we give Orr $200,000 a year, then what's left over for the other guys?" Well, hell, they may have to find some more for the other guys. Orr is the only player who can help the other teams out, and if I owned a team, I'd be happy to pay part of Orr's salary to see him signed. Like in Oakland, Orr played there on a Sunday night and they drew 10,500. St. Louis came there on a Wednesday, and they drew 3000. In Los Angeles Orr drew 12,700—a capacity house, only the second time in history they'd filled the rink, and the first time was when Orr was there last year—the next night against St. Louis they drew only 7,200. Vancouver's general manager says he could sell an extra 30,000 or 40,000 tickets when Orr is in town. Now, if I were the owner of Vancouver, and I knew I could get Orr in there three times a year and it was going to make an attendance difference of 8,000 a game, hell, I'd kick in $10,000 to Boston to sign Orr. Eight thousand people for three games at five bucks a pop, hell, that's $120,000. You're damn right I'd pay it, or at least put some heat on the Bruins to sign Bobby.

I tell you, his next contract is going to be the most exciting thing in sports. It will be at least five years. There's going to be enough security in it so that if he's injured or dies [sic] he will still have longterm protection. Bobby is going to go public. I wouldn't be a bit surprised if he became a stockholder in the Boston Garden. In my opinion he is entitled to a piece of every hot dog and bottle of beer sold above the average. Ten years from now Bobby will have at least a million tucked away, and if he wants, he'll be a part owner of a NHL franchise. And whatever he gets is going to reap benefits for every other player in the game. He has already changed hockey, and he's going to change it still more. . . .

Throughout it all Orr remains remote and circumspect, a little abashed at all the furor unloosed in his name, like some medieval monk whose pious lifework has inadvertently overturned the status quo of which he is a contented member.

"I was only fourteen when I was sold into servitude to Boston, so really, playing hockey is the only thing I've ever done." The blue eyes cloud over briefly as he ponders the look of that word *servitude* in print, and he adds:

> But don't get me wrong; I'm happy to be in servitude to Boston. Everyone is always telling me how I've changed the game. But the Players Association and the League expansion, which made it possible to televise the game nationally, have had more to do with players' getting more pay than I have. I hope players are getting more money now, but I can't see where I was responsible. Money. Everyone is asking me about money. Hell, I'm just one of the Bruins. I just try to do a job. I'm no different from a mechanic.

Just a simple mechanic-serf, who, with the help of his lawyer, froze over the Red Sea and led his people to the promised land of deferred payments, tax shelters, and six-figure contracts.

BASEBALL FEELS A PINCH [5]

Major-league baseball—the game that made national superheroes out of ordinary men like Tyrus Raymond Cobb, George Herman Ruth and Jack Roosevelt Robinson—today is being challenged as it has never been challenged before. As big-league ball enters its 102nd season, it no longer seems to fit the national mood. Worse, the men who run baseball show little inclination to adapt the sport to that changing mood.

The result is that in an era described as the Golden Age of Professional Sports, baseball finds itself in the fiscal doldrums. It has been shoved aside by football as the most popular and profitable professional game. In growth it is being thoroughly outclassed by such formerly minor pro-

[5] From "Who Says Baseball Is Like Ballet?" *Forbes.* 107:24-6+. Ap. 1, '71. Reprinted by permission of *Forbes* Magazine.

fessional sports as basketball, hockey, golf, bowling, auto racing and even tennis.

The grand old game has been groaning for some time, but it really seemed to come apart at the seams last year [1970]. "Baseball seemed to do everything it could to get itself into ill repute," says Bill Veeck, who in years past was baseball's greatest showman (he once hired a midget player to boost attendance) when he owned in succession the Cleveland Indians, the former St. Louis Browns and the Chicago White Sox.

First, last year there was the lawsuit of star outfielder Curt Flood that almost overshadowed the season itself. His suit, which may draw an appeals court decision this season, challenged baseball's exemption from the antitrust laws and its right to control forever where and for whom its players play. Then there was the damaging gambling association case of pitcher Denny McLain, whose wrist was only lightly tapped when Baseball Commissioner Bowie Kuhn suspended him for but half a season. As a fitting climax, Kuhn's own comments helped make a best-selling book out of *Ball Four*, ex-pitcher Jim Bouton's offhanded exposé of organized baseball. . . .

As the game now enters perhaps its most critical season, the fiscal problems are the ones that hurt most. Baseball has become big business. Based on data filed in the Curt Flood case, it is estimated that the two major leagues took in some $163 million last year in gate receipts, television revenues and concession income.

But if there is a lot of cash around the sport, there's very little profit. Despite a record attendance in 1970 of 28.7 million, the overall trend was bearish. As long ago as 1948—before television coverage and the expansion from 16 to 24 major-league teams—paid attendance was already 20.9 million. The American League drew 12.1 million fans in 1970; in 1948 the league drew 11.1 million. "And now they are playing with 50 percent more clubs and eight more games each year per club," Veeck notes.

In Trouble on the Home Screen

There's trouble, too, on the television side, which accounts now for fully 25 percent of baseball revenues. The ratings of the nationally televised Game of the Week peaked at 9.4 in 1967 (as measured by the A. C. Neilsen scale) and have declined every year since—to 8.1, a 14 percent drop. Baseball's star attraction, the annual World Series, has fallen even more, from a 1966 rating of 25.7 to 21.0 in 1970. NBC's three-year contract to televise both expires this year, and it will be interesting to see—now that the networks no longer enjoy the former large revenues from cigarette ads—how much baseball will be able to get the next time around. Last year all television rights brought the industry $38 million. With the ratings down, that will be hard to match.

One result of lagging attendance growth and poor TV ratings at a time of soaring player salaries is that major-league teams look decidedly unchipper at the bottom line. The World Champion Baltimore Orioles admit they couldn't have come close to their $345,000 net-profit figure last year (on revenues of $4.6 million) if they hadn't gotten into the World Series. The San Francisco Giants, loaded with player talent (including three stars making over $100,000 apiece), suffered an operating loss of $900,000 last year. In all, 11 major-league franchises out of 24 are known to be losing money, and several more are on the borderline. "What kind of an industry can you say it is when the total net income adds up to only $5 million?" asks Walter O'Malley, whose Los Angeles Dodgers continue to be one of baseball's few bright success stories.

It all brings to mind the parting comment of Thomas Dockerty as he returned to Scotland after trying unsuccessfully to establish big-time professional soccer in the United States a few years ago. "Baseball," said Dockerty, "will be dead in twenty years."

Perhaps Dockerty's claim is extreme. But there is no doubt that our traditional sport is in a lot of trouble. The red ink might not be so disturbing during an economic downturn if there weren't so many indications that the game is on a long ride downward in popularity, especially among the young. In earlier generations ballplayers were youthful heroes. Today the average adolescent turns away from Little League records at thirteen for hard-rock ones. "One of our greatest challenges," admits Robert O. Reynolds, co-owner with former movie cowboy Gene Autry of the California Angels, "is to attract more fans in their teens and early twenties."

The game seems to be losing its attraction for older generations too. Today's corporate executive turns pro football TV parties into an autumn ritual. But in the summer he puts more emphasis on taking his family boating or camping. Like the youth of the seventies, he's bored by the yawns and stretches of baseball.

The Louis Harris organization ran a nationwide sports popularity poll last year which showed that baseball trailed pro football in popularity for the second year in a row. "Football is king among the young, with basketball second and baseball third and being pushed by auto racing," said Harris. What was most revealing, perhaps, was that baseball had dropped a full 11 percentage points in popularity since 1968, while football had remained relatively even.

The poll didn't get much play on the sports pages. And it is true enough, as baseball buffs will tell you, that a larger percentage of the American public goes to baseball games today than purchased tickets fifty years ago. The real test, however, is how baseball is doing with its potential audience. A contrasting analysis by James Downs, president of the influential Real Estate Research Corporation, shows that in 1920, with sixteen major-league teams in ten cities, the ratio of patrons to possible ticket buyers was 61 percent. The ratio is now below 37 percent. Bill Veeck asks whether the New York Mets, even with a profitable attendance of 2.6 million, are really doing well in an area of 14 million people, when the Cincinnati Reds draw 1.8 million in a metropolitan area of 1.4 million?

In addition, the major-league clubs are still smarting over sparsely filled stands at last year's play-offs in Minneapolis and Pittsburgh.

Speeding Things Up

There is a business moral in all this. Downs and Veeck are just two of a number of critics who believe baseball managements are living in the past. "The owners transact business like this was the nineteenth century," says lawyer Marvin Miller, director of the Players Association. On the field they do a second-rate job of entertainment merchandising. Games can run from two and one half to three and one half hours and longer. They resist rule changes that would speed up the game. Basketball, on the other hand, has introduced the twenty-four-second rule, which makes the game faster with higher scoring. Tennis has introduced tie-breaker games to shorten matches. But baseball fans are treated to dragged-out games which run through a lengthy 162-game season. Michael Burke, president of the New York Yankees and a vice president of its owning corporation, the Columbia Broadcasting System, says that twenty-one teams suffered a 35 percent to 40 percent drop in attendance after Labor Day last year. He's pushing Kuhn for a much shorter major-league season, perhaps by as many as forty games.

What football managements have learned to do, Veeck believes, is sell the game itself as exciting. Even if a contest isn't for the Superbowl title, people will watch to plot the strategy, see a good pass or a bone-jarring tackle. Baseball, on the other hand, has sold the won-and-lost column. A team almost has to be in contention for the pennant to rate a good audience, and by July a majority of clubs are clearly out of the running.

The downward trend is partly the result of a sharp erosion in baseball's psychological appeal in our society. Syndicated psychologist Dr. Joyce D. Brothers, who also is a sports buff, contends that an organized sport depends tremendously on a general cultural priority. Today there is more of a demand for speed and violence. "Violence breeds a tolerance of violence and a desire for violence," she says. "Therefore, the attraction of football grows."

Running along with these cultural trends is the explosion in leisure-time sports for the individual. "I'm not so worried about the competitive sports as I am the struggle with other summer activities for the entertainment dollar," says Kuhn. Boating, camping, motorcycling, even frisbee tossing and boomeranging are riding popularity waves.

Yet to be fully assessed is the impact of television on baseball in the past twenty years. There are those who believe that TV broadcasters have made it a very different game indeed inside the American psyche. William O. Johnson, Jr., a *Sports Illustrated* editor, theorizes that a new sports era has, in fact, arrived. The new fan lives in his TV chair awaiting the next ersatz sports thrill but missing the commercials. At least that's the way Johnson pictures him in his book, *Super Spectator and the Electric Lilliputians.* He writes:

> This, in the Epoch of Super Spectator, is the way the mass of America takes its sports. . . . Insulated, isolated, miniaturized, in gloom of darkened room with essential plug in essential socket, the electronic window aglow, a kindly capitalist to pay the freight while Super Spectator coolly steps way from his set to go to the bathroom.

The joys of real viewing, the hot dogs, the beer, the roar of the crowd have succumbed to simulated viewing.

But is baseball paced to this kind of spectator sport? Paul Weiss, a professor of philosophy at Catholic University and author of *Sport,* thinks TV coverage has warped baseball badly. "It's not the real game. It's too slow and becomes just pitcher against batter. They ignore the interaction in the outfield. The spectator is being cheated." Some observers think NBC improved coverage last fall when it flashed close-ups, instant replays and split-screen movements during the World Series. But most fans are treated to plodding coverage by regional hookups that follow their home teams out of town. If the spectator is seeing something other than real baseball—and is bored by it—what impetus is there to rush out to the stadium when the home team returns for a series?

No Incentive

Despite all this, as the teams ran through the traditional six weeks of spring training this year in Florida and Arizona, the twenty-four major-league owners gave no hint the game might be on its deathbed. Most of the owners are wealthy individuals who like to be characterized as sportsmen. Only nine of the twenty-four are full-time owners, and several of them, such as Calvin E. Griffith of the Minnesota Twins, Robert Carpenter, who takes no salary as president of the Philadelphia Phillies, and Horace Stoneham of the San Francisco Giants, might best be termed sportsmen, too.

And that is probably the heart of the matter. Shorn of the profit motive by its sportsmen owners, baseball has been deprived of the necessity to tailor itself to the demands of its market—either at the stadium or on the television screen. (Philip Wrigley, for example, has steadfastly refused to install lights at his ball park so his Cubs could play home games at night, when attendance potential is far greater.) The result is that baseball does not really compete as other businesses do for the customers' dollars. Why should it? Their sportsmen owners are there to pick up the losses if need be.

"These are men who love the game," says Walter O'Malley, who won his millions by getting into baseball and moving the Dodgers from Brooklyn to Los Angeles. "They can stand to take a loss and they will. But they'd rather make a little money. And some of us would like to make a lot."

Baseball does offer some advantages financially through capital gains, or in tax write-offs on player contracts. O'Malley made $4 million plus, in one year, shortly after taking the Dodgers out of Brooklyn in 1958. The Pilots went into

Seattle as an expansion club in 1969 for $5.6 million. It cost Milwaukee interests $10.8 million to pick up the same team just a year later. But most owners don't have time for the day-to-day details of baseball. Therefore, they have turned most of the decisions over to general managers who have been in the game a long time. They are baseball men, like Frank Lucchesi, general manager of the Phillies, who have a vested interest in keeping the sport the way it has always been. Says O'Malley: "There are no new ideas in baseball. When someone comes up with an idea to revolutionize the game, it's usually something that's been dusted off from yesterday."

Though they operate their teams with a slightly better eye on balance sheets, the title of sportsman seems also to apply to those owners with large corporate involvements: August A. Busch, who enjoys the St. Louis Cardinals as an Anheuser-Busch subsidiary; Jerold C. Hoffberger who heads the National Brewing Company and the world champion Baltimore Orioles; Philip K. Wrigley, with his Chicago Cubs and a chewing gum fortune; Charles Bronfman of the Montreal Expos and the Seagram liquor empire; Robert A. Uihlein, president of Schlitz Brewing Company and an owner of the new Milwaukee Brewers; and also William Paley, chairman of CBS, whose Yankees have made money in only two of the six years CBS has had the team.

What do such men get out of baseball? Take Ewing M. Kauffman, whose fortune is built on pharmaceuticals but who, along with his wife, Muriel, has become a tremendous baseball fan now that he owns the Kansas City Royals. Kauffman says flatly that "anyone would be idiotic to go into baseball as an investment." Kauffman figures he has shot at least $15 million on the Royals since he took on the expansion team in 1968. He plunked down $6 million for the franchise, another $6 million to acquire six farm teams. He has put another $1.5 million into a year-round baseball academy he's started in Sarasota, Florida, and $5 million to help complete Kansas City's new baseball stadium. . . .

In Kansas City, Kauffman is now a hero. He saved major-league baseball for the city when insurance-man Charles O. Finley abruptly moved the Athletics (once of Philadelphia, remember?) to Oakland. And the new stadium will be his pride and joy. "We'll have a scoreboard ten stories high," he says. "A man knocks a home run, a computer will draw his face in lights. It will be the greatest scoreboard in the world." Before baseball, Kauffman was a drug salesman who had parlayed $4,300 in poker winnings into a $50 million interest in his Kansas City-based Marion Labs.

Other than public accolades and civic pride, it's hard to see what other owners like Thomas Yawkey, who poured a lumber fortune into Boston's Red Sox; or Mrs. Joan W. Payson, sister of publisher John Hay Whitney, who underwrote the New York Mets during seven unprofitable years, really get out of the game. It's hard to see also what they're doing to move the game forward.

Riding on a Roller Coaster

There are some indications the owners realize they're on a nationwide roller coaster going downward. Putting the Yankees on the block, as is now rumored, may signal that. Trucking executive Robert E. Short has indicated he would like to sell the Washington Senators, now suffering from lagging attendance. [The team was sold and became the Texas Rangers.—Ed.] NBC is reported to be interested in the moneymaking Los Angeles Dodgers. Only O'Malley hasn't heard about it, and there seem to be very few other buyers of baseball teams available.

It's not necessarily strike three for baseball. O'Malley believes the game still offers the cheapest ticket around (an average ducat is still only $2.50), and that if owners manage, trade and promote well, they'll make a profit. Burke of the Yankees is pressing for rule changes to speed up the game. And there is talk of splitting the two leagues into three divisions each, or of creating three eight-team leagues.

The idea in each case is to sharpen competition, cut some costs and provide for possible expansion to Dallas, Toronto, New Orleans and even Tokyo. Expansion also spreads new millions to present owners in payment for giving up players to new teams. But, says Joseph Durso, baseball writer for the New York *Times*, "Baseball is already overextended. The kill ratio of franchises is going to be high."

Can baseball win its way back into the cultural heart of America? Burke thinks that with its easier motions and its emphasis on the individual, baseball provides "an essential counterpoint to the nonindividual of today's frenetic society." Says Commissioner Kuhn: "These are some of the most highly skilled players you'll see in sports. It's almost an art form. Look at the rhythm, the geometry of the game. It's pleasing to the eye. It's almost like ballet."

Perhaps baseball can be marketed in the seventies as kind of a nostalgic art form. And perhaps it can even be sold that way over television to a specialized audience when, as O'Malley thinks is inevitable, a form of "moderate-cost pay cable television," moves into the sport. But unless some moneymaking zeal, the old discipline of profit and loss, is reinjected into the game, chances are that baseball's days as the great national sport are over.

Maybe our national pastime will end up just as novelist-essayist and baseball-lover Mark Harris hopes it will: as a minor sport, a quaint anachronism where the pitcher takes all day and home run kings step out of the batter's box to watch jet planes pass overhead.

THE HORSY SET [6]

Racing is big business, very big business. It is the largest spectator sport in the United States. Just to give you an example of how big it really is, over the Labor Day weekend of 1971 more than 842,000 people went out to the thirty-two

[6] From *Winning the Off-Track Bet*, by John Alden, a writer on racing and a keen judge of horses. Doubleday. '73. p 11-15. Copyright © 1973 by Doubleday & Company, Inc. Reprinted by permission of the publisher.

thoroughbred race tracks, which were in operation, and bet more than $64 million! That's a lot of money. Where does it all go?

Most of it goes right back to the bettors, but by no means all of it. Let's take New York State for example and Belmont Park in particular. There during that particular weekend, 91,708 fans wagered a total of $9,251,754. Out of that the state took more than $1 million and the New York Racing Association, the operator of Belmont Park, more than $600,000. Some individual bettors left with more than they came; some did not. As a whole, however, those 90,000-plus bettors left over $1.6 million at that one track on that one weekend. Truly, horse racing is the goose which lays the golden egg, if not for the individual then certainly for the state. How is this done? Through the magic of the pari-mutuel betting system under which all tracks in this country operate and have for approximately the last thirty years. *Parimutuel* literally means *mutual stake* in French. They started the whole thing. It's mutual in that the bettors who win get something back, so does the track operator and so does the state. But the state doesn't *bet* any money, so it can't lose!

In New York the law dictates that the track will receive 7 percent of all monies wagered (3 percent of which goes directly for purses for the winning horses). Including something called breakage, the state receives 11 percent more which goes into the general treasury and hopefully is returned to the taxpayers in the form of public services. That's a total of 18 percent. Every time you make a $2 wager you are contributing 36 cents to the New York Racing Association and the State of New York. Naturally, most people don't really think about this. They are primarily concerned with winning, but even when they win they're losing something. If, for instance, your horse comes in first, returning $5 for the $2 which you bet, had there been no takeout you would actually be entitled to a $6 return. The moral is obvious. It's more rewarding to be a politician than a horse player.

The Parimutuel Advantage

In theory, however, the parimutuel system has one distinct advantage. It removes the track operator and the government from having any interest in the outcome of any particular race. The amount of money which they make is determined only by how much is bet *not* by which horse wins. This goes a long way toward keeping things more honest. But this does not apply to the bookie. What keeps him in business depends entirely on whether or not he books more losing bets than winners. He takes all the money that is bet with him on various horses and pays back those who won at the same price (with certain exceptions) at which the track legally pays off its customers. Since he gets no percentage of the take, he is definitely interested in which horse wins any given race.

Even in a legal gambling casino in Nevada you are pitted directly against the management, the guy who owns the machines, the cards and the dice with which you are playing. He does not receive an established cut of each bet made but merely collects from losers and pays off winners. It is quite obvious that he has a vested interest in seeing that there are more losers than winners. Given man's capacity for avarice, this interest increases the likelihood that an individual operator *might* try to cheat the bettor so that he loses more. In the case of parimutuel betting, however, you may take some comfort in the fact that the track itself makes no more or less profit whether you win or lose, only on how much you bet.

Off-Track Betting

Here's where off-track betting [OTB] comes into the picture. [For a further discussion of this aspect of racing, see "Sports, Gambling, and the Public Interest," in Section VI, below.—Ed.] State and city governments need methods to raise more revenue. They know people like to gamble, and they in turn are gambling on the fact that if you offer people more opportunities to do so, they will take advantage of them.

The best way to start is to take an industry wherein gambling is already established and has been accepted by the public as a whole and work from there. Horse racing is a natural. What the politicians *say* they'd like to do is divert some of the billions of dollars that are bet illegally through bookies into legitimate channels, thereby making it less profitable for criminal syndicates and through taxation more beneficial to the general public. What really worries the track operators is that if you make it convenient to bet in town, it will divert many racing fans away from the track itself, thereby depriving the operators of the additional revenue derived from admissions, program sales, parking concessions, food and drink, etc. Also the track gets nowhere near the 7 per-cent piece of the action (in New York it is less than 2 per-cent) which off-track betting generates since they do not operate the betting establishments located downtown. At the present time their dismal warning is that if their attend-ance figures suffer, they will no longer be able to offer attractive purse money, the quality of racing in general will suffer, fewer people will bet less money, and everyone will lose.

Off-track proponents claim that this dismal prediction is nonsense. Their new betting arrangement will actually stimulate business, not only by attracting money which is now being bet illegally through bookies but by developing *new* customers, people who formerly would not bet at all since they couldn't take time to go out to the track and would not associate themselves with the illegal stigma of betting through bookies. They further state that these new customers are likely to become so enthralled with the sport that they too will start going out to the track in person on their days off, something they had never done before.

The bookies claim they aren't worried at all. They say that much of their money comes from bets on other sports than horse racing, baseball, football, basketball, etc. Further-more, they offer an even more personalized service for people who can't afford to spend the time standing in line at a legal betting parlor. All bookies employ runners who go right to the customer to take his bet. Many of them will take bets of less than two dollars, the minimum which you can wager. Some even give credit, something no track ever does.

At the present time it is impossible to tell who is really correct. The tracks are worried, but their attendance figures do not as yet indicate any cause for concern. OTB, which is hardly off the ground, opens new shops every week and handles several hundred thousand dollars daily. The bookies claim that with them it's business as usual. At this writing, eight state legislatures have various proposals before them for the establishment of betting facilities away from the tracks themselves. Another dozen have committees studying the feasibility of various systems. Almost all the rest are watching ... and waiting.

One *sure* bet (occasionally there are such things)—legalized off-track betting is no longer a thing of the past. It is here, and in one form or another it is here to stay.

THE LUCRATIVE GOLF BUSINESS [7]

In the past ten or fifteen years, golf has ceased to be simply a popular sport and has taken on some of the attributes of an industry generating financial returns of a size once found only in business proper. How did it happen to a game that non-golfers find dull in the extreme? The key lies in the psychological makeup of the golf fan, an uncomfortable base for an industry, but one that nowadays is not that unusual.

The typical golf fan is a player himself and identifies to an extraordinary degree with the tournament professionals he sees on television. What the fan sees done by Arnold Palmer or Jack Nicklaus or Tony Jacklin ..., he wants to do too, and from time to time he does. ... [Charts show]

[7] From "The £2 Billion Golf Business." *Economist.* 236:50-1. Jl. 11, '70. Reprinted by permission.

average performances but there is hardly a golfer living who has not sunk a 30-foot putt or chipped the ball stiff to the pin, or even blasted a drive more than 250 yards down the centre of the fairway. The difference between the amateur and the professionals is that they do consistently what he does once in a season, but the fact that he does it at all establishes an emotional bond that does not exist between the amateurs and the experts in other sports. Golf is a difficult game and skill, even on a high amateur level, is attainable by only a small percentage of the people who play it. So the typical golfer is frustrated but fascinated.

Multiply these feelings by twenty million or so and the result is a dynamic world-wide market. The number of players has doubled or trebled in some countries since the 1950s. Growth would have been even greater except for a shortage of golf courses, particularly in Japan. In the United States alone, the game has 12 million followers, nearly 10 million of whom play at least fifteen times a year. There are an estimated 2 million golfers in Japan, while uncounted others, with no access to a course, devotedly bash balls on driving ranges.

In Britain, only 750,000 people belong to clubs but as many again play often enough to be considered golfers. Perhaps a further 500,000 play a round or two once or twice a year, giving a rough total of 2 million. Golf is also popular through most parts of the British Commonwealth and in the past few years has begun to catch on in continental countries, notably France and Spain.

The twenty million more or less serious amateurs make up a huge market, because golf, an ideal sport for consumption-oriented societies, demands reasonably expensive equipment. A new set of clubs costs upwards of £100 [£1 is worth about $2.40.—Ed.] and then there are golf balls—120 million a year in Britain—bags, shoes, clothing, gloves, trolleys [carts], and club membership fees. The average British golfer keeps his clubs five years or longer, compared with the more model-conscious American player who buys a new set every few years, but even so it is hard to see golfers anywhere spending less than £50 a year on the sport, and the world average has been put nearer £100 especially if you include the cost of food and drink at clubs. That adds up to between £1 billion and £2 billion laid out by golfers each year, on the assumption that club dues work out at £15 or £20. This is becoming a low figure even for Britain. In the United States, dues often run upwards of ten times higher. The estimate for total spending is, therefore, conservative.

Why They Spend It

Part of golf's popularity is rational. It can be taken up fairly late in life, after the children have grown up and when there is more money to spare. It can be played almost to the grave. It is an outdoor game in pleasant countrified surroundings, making a refreshing break for urban man. A sophisticated handicapping system, allowing golfers of widely differing abilities to compete with each other in meaningful terms, strengthens the social attractions, which are of considerable importance at many clubs. So is the sense of status that golf peculiarly confers on its devotees in some parts of the world, most notably in Japan and the United States, where playing golf is often taken as a sign of business success. On the other hand, in Scotland, where the game originated, it was and still is a sport for working men, and, particularly on municipally owned courses, it is still geared to working-class incomes. A visitor can play a round at St. Andrews, the most famous championship course for 12s. 6d. [about $1.50] during the week.

The recent growth of golf cannot, however, be explained on wholly rational grounds. It owes much to television and to a single individual, Arnold Palmer, a remarkable man and golfer who not only won an impressive number of championships in the late 1950s and early 1960s, but did so in a dramatic, come-from-behind fashion, often making nearly impossible shots in critical situations. More important, he was temperamentally different from most other golf champions, who reacted . . . [stony-faced] to crowds and competitive pressure. Arnold Palmer liked crowds and the crowds, at the tournament and in front of the television screens, felt and responded to this. Although Palmer has not won many championships in the past few years, "Arnie's Army" of fans almost always outnumber the crowds following other tournament leaders. He is easy to identify with. Mr. Mark McCormack, Palmer's manager (and many another champion's, including Tony Jacklin) likes to quote the analysis of psychologist Dr. Ernest Dichter:

> People see themselves winning through Palmer. He looks and acts like a regular guy, and at the same time he does the kinds of things others wish they could do. His expressiveness makes his spectators feel that they are part of his game; he looks as though he needs their help, and they respond.

Just before Palmer's first big win in 1957, there were actually fewer golf courses in the United States than there were at the end of the war. By last year [1969], the number had shot up from 5,500 to nearly 10,000, and the number of golfers had more than doubled.

Because Palmer has had such a big effect on golf generally, it is likely that the rise of Tony Jacklin will spur the growth of the game in Britain. Jacklin is Britain's first world-class golfer since the 1930s. Last year he won the British Open, a feat that has been worth £230,000 to him over and above the actual prize money. When this was followed by the US Open championship a few weeks ago, this removed any doubts that last year's British win could have been a fluke. Jacklin's earnings from his American win cannot be calculated at this stage, but should make him a sterling millionaire. Already his fee for personal appearances has reportedly risen to £3,000 a day. Jacklin does not possess Palmer's superb personality, but he is a good and chatty mixer, and any man who can leave a $21,000 cheque in his pocket is going to endear himself to a British public starved for a British-born golf hero: the Yanks have dominated the game too long.

Professional Business

Palmer not only popularised golf beyond anything even imagined twenty or thirty years ago—total prize money in the United States in 1941 was roughly $177,000; last year it was nearly $6 million—he also found new ways of capitalising on his own popularity. Golfers and other athletes have long received income from endorsing commercial products, playing in exhibition matches, writing books and making personal appearances, but Palmer and McCormack, a former Cleveland lawyer started by Palmer in the management business, were probably the first to view a sports personality as a corporation unto himself and to conduct his business affairs as if he were a corporation. It was not just that Palmer and McCormack formed an actual corporate structure with subsidiary companies to handle Palmer's interests—the Palmer companies now have an annual payroll of about £800,000—but they viewed the Palmer personality as a product to sell as much as if it were a manufactured article. Golf products were obvious articles to endorse, but the business did not stop there. After a time, the two realised the Palmer name could sell a great many things unconnected with golf. McCormack set out their business philosophy in a book where he explained that

If two dry-cleaning shops are going to open in the same block and one is called Arnold Palmer's and the other is Irv Schlepperman's, it is the Palmer shop that has the best chance to succeed. You do not have any reason to think Arnold can wash your shirts, but you do know he excels at golf, has a reputation for being the best and seems like a familiar friend. Irv you simply don't know. So, given a choice, you are likely to try Palmer. It is by such small margins that new businesses survive.

It does not always work. The long-playing "Arnold Palmer Presents Music for Swingin' Golfers" flopped, and there were other mishaps. Photographers invited to watch

Palmer demonstrate a practice net he was endorsing saw him blast a hole straight through it. But the failures have been rare. There has been a two-way payoff. The advertising of products with golfers' names and faces attached has done a great deal to promote golf. In the process, golf has been changed, particularly in the United States where more advertising money is spent on golf than anywhere else. Here the equation of golf with mass-produced consumer products has helped wash away much of the snobbery and exclusiveness of the sport in the United States, although a perceptive man would not have to travel far in that country to discover places where they still hold sway. Less attractive are the subliminal advertising techniques becoming associated with the game. There is nothing wrong with an airline using a golf star to advertise its services or a shirt company announcing that he wears its shirts. Implied in all these advertisements is the fact that the star has received a substantial fee for appearing. But the newer technique is to see that the star just happens to be wearing the right shirt, and that he leaves the right airline bag lying around when he meets photographers at the end of a triumphant game. The sponsor no longer seeks to advertise his connection with the star, and is in fact nowhere to be seen.

The Price of Commercial Exploitation

The promotional side of tournament golf sometimes threatens to overwhelm the game itself. Mark McCormack jammed so many events into Jacklin's schedule in the sixteen days between Jacklin's winning the US Open and the start of the British Open that Jacklin had little time to practise at St. Andrews. Also, he looked so tired the day before the Open began that some golf writers gave him little chance to repeat his triumph. Jacklin promptly confounded his critics by shooting a 29 for the first nine holes of the Open, the lowest outward half ever achieved in any event at St. Andrews. But the critics still seemed to have a point. Jacklin is only twenty-six and apparently he can stand up to this kind of treatment. A few years ago Palmer, a physically powerful man, could also take whatever routine commercial exploitation could set for him. But the constant pressure of work is perhaps one reason why Palmer's game has lost its fine edge. From tee to green, Palmer is still the finest golfer in the world but when he is on the green he is a different class of golfer entirely. In his heyday, he was deadly at sinking eight- and ten-foot putts for birdies. Now he seldom sinks anything but short putts.

Advertising men prefer some golfers to others because they want certain personality traits associated with the products they are selling. Colgate-Palmolive, for instance, signed Jacklin to promote Rapid-Shave in Britain before he had won the British Open. They regarded him as a promising young golfer but they were more interested in the youth and energy he radiated. Such considerations are fine for the extroverts of the game but the introvert is likely to find himself relatively anonymous no matter how many tournaments he wins. Bill Casper and Gene Littler are cases in point. Many golf writers will argue that Casper and Littler play golf as well as Mark McCormack's Big Three—Palmer, Gary Player and Jack Nicklaus—but they have never achieved anything like the fame. This situation might hurt golf eventually as golfers tailor their personalities to suit the advertising men. Gone will be the moody players, the angry club-throwers and the loudmouths who insult the stuffy officials who still run the game in many places. Gone with them will be much of the colour of golf. Just possibly some fans may decide that the game is not that interesting after all.

II. COMMERCIALISM

EDITOR'S INTRODUCTION

That sports is a business one must concede. That sports and business are closely allied in America, that they feed each other's needs and cater to each other's demands is quite another aspect of the problem. Yet it cannot be denied that sports in America today are exploited for commercial purposes and that sportsmen themselves—owners, players, even the fans, to a large extent—appear to revel in the process. Examples of this range far and wide. They include cities that build multimillion-dollar stadiums to attract sports teams and house them virtually rent-free (all with the hearty approval of the Chamber of Commerce), and they include baseball players who, for a few hundred dollars, lend their names and portraits to bubblegum manufacturers who want to appeal to the nation's sports-happy youth. They include the top-notch salesman whose outstanding performance is rewarded with a trip to the Superbowl or the World Series, and they include, at the amateur level, the college-bound athlete who is bribed with sports cars and new wardrobes to lend his abilities on behalf of old State U.

This section is designed to explore the sometimes seamy, sometimes amusing, always fascinating, role of commercialism in modern American sports. In the first article a sports writer for the Baltimore *Sun* summarizes the quest for the "fast buck" which, he indicates, may be sounding the death knell of professional athletics in the United States. In their contempt for the loyalty of the old-fashioned fan, he says, club owners may be cutting their own throats.

The second article provides a revealing portrait of the front-row seat provided to business at that annual rite of pro football, the Superbowl. Rarely has the commercial alliance between sports and business generally been captured so effectively and revealingly. Though the article that follows—examining the link between bubblegum and baseball —proceeds in a lighter vein, the underlying message is almost as startling. This particular spinoff from the business of sports, it turns out, involves a full-time team of scouts, photographers, artists, and statisticians just to keep those baseball-bubblegum cards up to date and accurate.

The fourth article describes, among other things, the effort of the Washington Senators (now the Texas Rangers) to raise home attendance by passing out free pantyhose to the ladies. Of a more serious and disturbing nature are the last two contributions. One describes the dollar windfall that Baltimore expected from its reputation as the "city of champions," while the other, by a staff reporter of the *Wall Street Journal*, tells us that the old and (it was hoped) forgotten practice of luring high school athletic stars through material bribes from colleges and universities is neither gone nor, alas, forgotten.

PRO IS FOR PROFITS [1]

Last spring [1971], the Atlanta Hawks professional basketball team finished its grueling and disappointing eighty-two-game schedule with ten more defeats than victories. Time to put away their equipment? Indeed not. Despite their losing record over the previous five months, the Hawks joined seven other "outstanding" teams in a new, trumped-up series of forty playoff games which would eventually decide the National Basketball Association's championship.

Thanks to their faithful fans, the Chicago Black Hawks are the most profitable team in professional hockey. Yet last year those same fans were not permitted to see the national telecast of the Hawks' final championship game. One reason

[1] From "In Pro Sports, the Dollar Is King," by Bill Surface, sportswriter for the Baltimore *Sun*. *Reader's Digest*. 100:146-9. Mr. '72. Reprinted with permission from the March 1972 *Reader's Digest*. Copyright 1972 by The Reader's Digest Assn., Inc. Condensed from Baltimore *Sunday Sun*.

may be that Arthur Wirtz principal owner of the Black
Hawks, also happens to have an interest in a Chicago theater
which charged fans $7 each to see a closed-circuit telecast
of the game.

Whether it is basketball or hockey—or baseball or football—owners of professional clubs today are demonstrating a
far greater appetite for the fast dollar than for legitimate
competition. The commercialism has become so cynical,
many fans feel, that it seriously threatens the integrity of all
professional athletics. How long can sports survive, they ask,
when the more loyalty we show, the more we are exploited.

Examples of such exploitation are endless. A majority
of the twenty-six pro football teams *require* season-ticket
holders to buy tickets for meaningless, late-summer practice
games—or else forfeit their right to hard-to-get regular-season
tickets. The Massachusetts attorney general recently ruled
the tactic illegal in that state, but teams elsewhere have continued—and even sharpened—this technique. Before anyone
was eligible to buy a single season-ticket for the 1971 Dallas
Cowboys' home-games, he first had to purchase a bond
which, in many instances, will not mature until the year
2008! A fan who bought $1000 worth of bonds qualified for
one seat between the 30-yard lines. But a $250 bond ($290
on the installment plan) usually landed him in a corner or
end zone.

Subsidized by the Taxpayer

Profiteering from sports is now so extensive that even
persons who never watch a game suffer—through higher
taxes. Although a team's veterans are systematically replaced
by younger players, the club owner is allowed to deduct
from his Federal income taxes a mythical value for the "depreciation" of the older players' contracts. If a team was
purchased for $10 million, say, the owner could deduct prac-
tically the entire sum from the tax on the team's profits over
a period of three to seven years (providing there has been a
major player turnover). If he sells his team, then the new
owner can, in turn, depreciate players' contracts.

This tax loophole, plus a guaranteed income from broad-casting rights and hefty fees for allowing new teams into their leagues, makes it difficult for established, properly financed teams to lose money. Despite having the smallest stadium and the worst record in pro football, the New England Patriots earned $500,000 in 1970 *after* deductions for players' contract depreciation. Moreover, the value of most franchises has increased phenomenally; even the *un*-successful Philadelphia Eagles, purchased for $5.5 million in 1963, were resold for $16.1 million in 1969.

While quietly avoiding taxes, many a club owner piously brandishes his ostensible operating losses as a reason for transferring his team unless he gets lower rent or a better (read "bigger") stadium. By shrewdly publicizing his search for a new home, an owner can pressure the team's city into underwriting a new public stadium or arena. Under urgent "deadlines," the cost is usually left to the mercy of an en-tangled web of contractors sometimes affiliated with owners of other clubs. As a result, many of the two dozen public stadiums built or planned in the last ten years have suffered scandals. Before the blueprints were finished for a domed stadium in Buffalo, New York, for example, the projected minimum cost had risen from $50 million to $72 million, and two county legislators had been convicted of conspiracy to accept bribes. The plan for the stadium was later scrapped.

Such publicly financed stadiums are built with the prom-ise of generating vast new income for revenue-starved munic-ipalities, through increased hotel and restaurant business, and the like. But, in order to get this, taxpayers almost in-variably end up subsidizing both the stadium and the teams that use it. For example, the combined rental paid by Wash-ington's football Redskins and baseball Senators was so low that not once in the stadium's ten-year history did it cover even half the annual *interest* of $831,611 on the stadium's debt. But the stadium's administrators have been in a bind when it comes to reducing the annual $736,000 deficit; the Redskins' thirty-year lease forbids any other football team to play there.

Still, the Redskins' terms have been more equitable than those formerly demanded by the Senators, who charged the league's highest ticket prices and put on one of the most inept performances. By the end of the 1971 season, the Senators still hadn't paid half their 1970 rent. Instead, the owner, trucking [and] hotel magnate Robert E. Short, lobbied to have Congress establish his rent at *$1* a year and, in essence, give him nearly all income, during the baseball season, from the stadium's concessions, parking fees and billboards. When Congress refused, Short got his terms anyway—by moving the team to a suburb of Dallas. Once again, the only real losers were the fans.

Not even the phenomenal profits of some clubs can free taxpayers from subsidizing them. Baseball's most prosperous team, the New York Mets, frequently exercises a clause in its thirty-year lease which prevents virtually all other attractions from using city-owned Shea Stadium when the Mets are on the road. Even with rental revenues from the seven football games played after the Mets release Shea Stadium in mid-October, New York City has still had to spend an average of $300,000 a year—approximately $2.2 million since the stadium opened in 1964—to maintain it for the Mets. During this period, the Mets earned an estimated $9 million in profits, and the value of the franchise increased by $10 million.

Controlling TV Rights

As if the dollar-squeezing schemes of some owners weren't enough, they have also become the calculated policy of entire leagues. Consider the National Football League, which for years was governed by a Supreme Court ruling that it was subject to Federal anti-trust laws. This decree rankled club owners, mainly because it would invite lawsuits if the NFL absorbed a rival league and then attempted to control television rights for the entire sport. In 1966, NFL Commissioner Pete Rozelle persuaded Senator Russell Long (Democrat, Louisiana), who was then the Senate whip, and [the late] Representative Hale Boggs (Democrat, Louisiana), the House whip—both of whom were anxious to get a football team for their home-state constituents—to have Congress change the law.

The pleased club owners promptly awarded New Orleans an NFL team—and the league got a private law exempting it and the rival AFL from anti-trust charges in a proposed merger of the two leagues. (In effect, this exemption freed the league to ban home telecasts—a key device in the owners' battle to drum up more paying customers.)

This "exemption" was literally flaunted during the 1971 Superbowl. To obtain the game for its Orange Bowl, the city of Miami had to spend nearly $500,000 for promotion and the construction of 4,500 additional seats. Disregarding the majority of the taxpayers who underwrote this expense (and the fact that the game was announced as a sell-out), the NFL then prohibited the telecast of the game within a radius of seventy-five miles of Miami and sold the 79,204 tickets for $15 each—with all but a few thousand going to persons who had bought season tickets to the Miami Dolphins' home games or to persons somehow affiliated with the league's other teams.

A growing number of legislators contend that such blackouts, when all tickets are already sold, are illegal and unethical. Insists Senator William Proxmire (Democrat, Wisconsin): "The typical fan's taxes support both the stadium and the team. But, because of manipulation, he has no chance to see even one home game over the airwaves, which belong to the public—*not* to the NFL."

Sadly, instead of braking the trend toward more and more commercialism, many owners advocate a policy that automatically accelerates it. Under the guise of giving their sport "nationwide representation," they actively encourage the selling of additional team franchises. The result of such expansion is twofold: the established owners get richer, because each would-be owner must pay them as much as $10 million for the marginal players used initially to operate a team; the quality of competition (and the fan's enjoyment) is lowered, because there are only so many first-rate athletes. Thus, there is little doubt that the number of major-league teams, which has doubled in the past ten years, will continue to grow. "Doesn't all this league expansion look like a steal?" one owner admits with a gleeful smile.

The appeal of professional sports cannot continue unless realistic owners move vigorously to bring their greedy colleagues under effective control. As one fan bristled, after losing a lawsuit to lift the local blackout of a televised football game: "Someday enough fans will show these leagues that they can't come into a city, take the public's money, tell them to go to hell, and still maintain that they're running a clean, respectable sport. If the owners don't police themselves soon, it may be too late."

THE BIG SELL [2]

Because he succeeded in placing 96 floor displays of freeze-dried coffee, 21 over his six-week quota, in the food markets in his New York-New Jersey territory, Don Harris and his wife, Ellen, won a weekend trip to see Superbowl VII.

In his own humble way, Mr. Harris, a tall, solemn man of thirty-five who wears a red blazer with a Taster's Choice emblem embroidered in gold on the breast pocket, symbolizes the perfect marriage of sport and commerce that the National Football League's championship game has become.

From the nation's No. 1 fan, President Nixon, down through the gradations of corporate hierarchies, millions of men find emotional resonances between their own business lives and the grinding preparation of pro football, its crunch-

[2] From "Business in a Front Seat for Today's Super Bowl," by Tom Buckley, staff reporter. New York *Times.* p 1+. Ja. 14, '73. © 1973 by The New York Times Company. Reprinted by permission.

ing competition, its specialization, its team play and, most of all, its uncertainty.

"It's not so different from building a winning team," Mr. Harris, whose territory is in Rockland County, New York, and Bergen County, New Jersey, said . . . in his motel, set in a featureless landscape near the crossing of two freeways. "We didn't even use to be considered a contender but Taster's Choice got out in front nationwide in two and a half years and we're going to stay there."

So extensive are the commercial ties to the league—television contracts, promotional schemes, sales incentive contests, football competitions for boys—that something like 10,000 of the 90,182 seats for the game . . . at the Los Angeles Coliseum, including many of the best ones, will be occupied by men with such connections.

President Nixon, though he is a fervent Redskins rooter, will not attend the game. George Allen, the team's coach, said the President had told him why. "He said that when he went to a game it meant that about 100 tickets have to be made available for his security and the official party and so on, and he said that in a game of this magnitude he didn't want to deprive other fans of the tickets."

At the summit this year [1973] are Robert W. Sarnoff, the chairman of the RCA Corporation, and Julian Goodman, the president of its subsidiary, the National Broadcasting Company, who will sit with Pete Rozelle, the league president, in his box on the 50-yard line.

Biggest Sports Audience

Their network, which alternates with the Columbia Broadcasting System in presenting the big game, will carry it on 267 stations to an expected 75 million viewers, which would be the largest sports audience in history.

Also sitting near Mr. Rozelle will be the executives of the Chrysler Corporation, which alternates with the Ford Motor Company as the prime sponsor of the Superbowl. Chrysler has purchased four of the twenty minutes of national commercial time available during the game telecast. The standard rate is $200,000 a minute, but Chrysler, as a volume advertiser, is getting it for something less than that.

In addition, local stations are permitted to sell four minutes of commercial time of their own.

At WNBC-TV in New York, the going rate, according to a spokesman, is $7,500 for a thirty-second spot, which can be conveniently dropped into the forty-five-second period available between plays.

People in the industry estimate that, all told, nationwide television advertising expenditures for the game will be at least $10 million.

Chrysler has also brought 267 dealers, who were winners of sales incentive contests, and their wives to the Superbowl. Ford, which not by chance is having a vast sales meeting at Las Vegas this week, will fly in 650 of its best men for the game tomorrow.

For Fred Pollack, the manager of a Dodge dealership in Washington, it was a third straight Superbowl trip. "They raise our quota every year, but we just keep beating it," he said, sipping Scotch with his slim blonde wife, Sylvia, and Seymour J. Wulbert, another winning manager from Detroit.

"We met Sy and his wife in New Orleans last year and they were such fun people that we invited them to our daughter's wedding," said Mr. Pollack, a pudgy, bespectacled man of forty-five who wears his hair a good deal longer than Dodge dealers usually do.

"I call myself the hippy auto dealer on our radio commercials," he remarked.

"We moved 350 cars from October 10 to December 20," Mr. Pollack said. "I have eight salesmen and I gave them a $500 bonus if they sold twelve cars, and from there it went on up. The owners of the dealership do even better. They're going to Acapulco for five days in February."

Winning the sales contest, Mr. Pollack said, fills him with a sense of accomplishment, but even if he had not won, he said he probably would have come to the game since he is a fanatical Redskins fan.

"Everyone I know is," he said. "There's nothing like it. Pro football is the national pastime now. You really get action. Baseball is too slow."

Besides the television sponsors, their advertising agencies and public relations experts, the league also makes seats available to the scores of companies with which it has promotional tie-ins.

One of the most important of these clients is Sears, Roebuck and Company, which sells shirts, athletic jackets and equipment, sweaters and pajamas and also "youth room products" such as bedspreads, pennants and posters—all emblazoned with the symbols of the twenty-six pro football clubs.

"It's an unbelievable business," said Phil Read, Sears's assistant national retail sales manager. "The goods appeal to the boy, to the mother and to the dad who tends to say, 'I want my rugged little boy to show he roots for the Miami Dolphins,' or whatever team it is." . . .

Robert J. Bell, an official of the league's licensing agency, said that the purpose of the promotional arrangements was not to make money but "to expand and enhance the image of pro football."

"Our fee from each account is a flat $20,000 a year, which I think you could say is nominal," Mr. Bell said, "and if we do have a surplus it goes into a charitable foundation. Our interest in this is that the boy with the pennant on the wall of his room of today is the season-ticket buyer of tomorrow."

A display of products set up at a downtown hotel here showed that the range is wide indeed.

The Shell Oil Company offers a free tumbler decorated with an NFL club emblem with the purchase of eight gallons of gasoline. It gave out 17 million of the tumblers last year.

Sunoco builds traffic at its service stations with NFL Action Player Stamps that, it says, "are great to collect and trade." It also offers an album at 89 cents—a deluxe model costs $2.49—to paste them in.

Lum's, the quick-food franchiser, has been offering what is called in the trade a self-liquidating premium, which means that the 59 cents it charges for a thermal mug covers the cost of the item.

Commercial Typecasting

The players whose images adorn such goods are not expected to be acting only for the good of the game.

The fees are substantial for Don Shula, the Dolphins' coach, who speaks up on television for the Sunoco stamps, or for Dick Butkus of the Chicago Bears, who has been typecast in such commercials as an unrestrained beast of the gridiron, Bubba Smith of the Baltimore Colts as a genial giant, Joe Namath, the Jets' quarterback, as a man about town, or Fran Tarkenton of the Minnesota Vikings, who more typically of quarterbacks, is seen as a brisk executive type.

Many players in the twenty-four clubs that did not reach the championship will attend the game, a few for pleasure but most of them in the interests of business.

Al Atkinson, a Jets linebacker, who is a partner in a travel agency in his native Philadelphia, arranged a charter flight of 129 fans for a package price of $299 apiece.

"Mostly they're hard-up Eagles rooters who wait all year to see a good game," the baby-faced Mr. Atkinson said as he lifted a glass with several of his clients.

Where had the tickets, which are supposed to be more precious than pearls, come from, he was asked.

"Well, it's not what you know, it's who you know," he replied cryptically.

The allocation of Superbowl tickets is strictly controlled, up to a point.

The Los Angeles Rams, the team that regularly plays in the Coliseum, got 30,000 tickets, all of which went to its season-ticket holders. The Washington and Miami clubs got 12,000 each, and these went to season-ticket holders, too. The other clubs in the league got 800 each for a grand total of 73,200.

This left about 17,000 seats available. A league spokesman said that 8,000 to 10,000 were sold quietly in pairs to anyone who asked for them, an assertion that many persons close to the game find difficult to take seriously. The balance went to the league's commercial accounts, politicians and other public potentates of the sort who find it culturally imperative to be at a heavyweight championship fight, the Kentucky Derby or the seventh game of a World Series.

One such figure is Jimmy (The Greek) Snyder, the Las Vegas odds-maker, who has installed the Redskins as a three-point favorite.

"This is where the action is, "Mr. Snyder said ebulliently as he held open house in his $475-a-day, six-room suite at the Beverly Wilshire hotel.

In addition to handicapping, Mr. Snyder also operates a thriving public relations business and has just been signed to do a television commercial for Edge shaving cream.

"I've gotten 100 tickets for my friends and clients and now I need 32 more," he said, shaking his head in mock desperation. "The calls keep coming in."

Although sixty thousand persons have traveled here for the game, they scarcely cast a shadow in the vast inchoate expanse of greater Los Angeles. Their hotels are spread out in a fifty-mile radius from what could be described as the center of the city if it had one.

And while many residents of the city are rooting fundamentally for the Redskins whose coach, George Allen, and many of whose stars used to play for the Rams, there are a significant number who take no notice of the event.

At the Self Realization Fellowship Lake Shrine in Santa Monica, Brother Dharmananda, who in an earlier incarnation was known as Harold Culver and played high school football at Tallahassee, Alabama, said that he would be too busy with services to watch the game.

"People come from far and wide to seek peace here," he said.

CASHING IN ON CELEBRITY [3]

On the playing field, some professional athletes are worth millions. But on cardboard, they cost only a penny, which is one reason why bubble-gum card collecting is a favorite pastime of American youngsters.

Baseball cards, which date back to the 1880s, are the oldest and most popular sports cards. They disappear from countertops at a rate of 250 million each year.

Cashing in on this booming business is the Topps Chewing Gum Company which has expanded its operation to include basketball, football, hockey, soccer, and assorted novelty cards.

The company maintains a plant in Duryea, Pennsylvania, where the cards and gum are actually manufactured. But the brain trust and real heart of the business is in its Brooklyn, New York, headquarters.

Sy Berger, Topps's sports director, emphasizes that the firm is in the "children's entertainment business." Its cards bring the big leaguers to life with full-color pictures on one side of the card, and with loads of facts and figures on the other.

[3] From "On Bubblegum and Baseball," by Ross Atkin, staff correspondent. *Christian Science Monitor*. 65:1. F. 26, '73. Reprinted by permission from *The Christian Science Monitor*. © 1973 The Christian Science Publishing Society. All rights reserved.

"I've never seen kids so up on everything," Mr. Berger says of today's youngsters. "They study and learn the statistics. And if there is a mistake—boom—right away we're swamped with letters."

Part of Topps's success can be attributed to the completeness of the card sets. Each player who makes it in the majors comes rolling off the patented printing press at the Duryea plant. The same number of cards is printed of each player so every collector has an equal chance of getting the top stars.

Baseball cards have the advantage of being marketed during the summer months, the peak sales period for bubble gum. But this only partially accounts for their popularity.

Kids can envision baseball players as being one of them easier than they can identify with the monsters playing football or the giants playing basketball [Mr. Berger explains]. And instead of moving up and down a court or field en masse, baseball players can be singled out in the field or at the plate. A youngster can study a player's batting stance, how he wears his cap, even what he looks like—then go out and copy it all.

Designs Guarded

The design of the latest-model cards is always kept a secret even though the king of the card enterprises is not faced with stiff competition. Through the years, sports cards have come with everything from dog food to cereal, but Topps has held exclusive rights to the trade in the confectionery field since 1951.

As the business has grown, more teamwork has been needed among the 150 employees to produce the cards. There are scouts tracking down tomorrow's major leaguers, photographers taking their pictures, artists and statisticians assembling the product, and marketing experts studying how to improve and sell it.

Topps's own scouts are responsible for signing promising minor leaguers, who upon making the big leagues sign $250 contracts worth some $400 in wholesale merchandise.

Three full-time photographers infiltrate training camps, armed with all the latest equipment. Before the turn of the century, the players stood stiffly before flash-powder cameras swinging at a ball suspended from a string. Today, a staff of artists keeps busy producing eye-pleasing card formats. They choose color portraits and action shots from what is probably the most extensive sports picture file anywhere.

Two statisticians sort through the endless stream of batting and earned-run averages, RBI [runs batted in] totals, hometowns, etc. Conflicting information must be investigated for the sake of accuracy—a source of pride with Topps. Many sports broadcasters trust the cards enough to carry them as ready references.

Despite an enviable record for accuracy, Topps occasionally fouls things up. In 1969 the California Angels' batboy appeared on a card instead of third-baseman Aurelio Rodriguez, one of several cases of mistaken identity through the years.

Players have been known to tarnish the reputation, too. One year a mischievous Warren Spahn coaxed pitching mate Lew Burdette to wear his glove on his throwing hand during a picture-taking session. The discrepancy went undiscovered until the card hit the market. As a preventive measure, Topps now supplies its photographers with information on how a player bats and throws.

GIMMICKS AND GIVEAWAYS [4]

It took the Devil himself to pull the Washington Senators out of the hole in the musical *Damn Yankees*, and many an old-fashioned fan is wondering if the national capital's ball club [now the Texas Rangers] hasn't gone to the Devil again. What has the traditionalists upset is the dazzling array of gaudy giveaways and special events being used to promote the team's games. It's all very well, the traditionalists mut-

[4] From "Promotion: Selling the Senators." *Newsweek.* 76:82. Jl. 13, '70. Copyright Newsweek, Inc. 1970, reprinted by permission.

ter, to lure kids to the park with free bats, balls and baseball caps. But pantyhose?

"That was a hell of an idea," insists the Senators' public-relations chief, Oscar Molomot, who has handed out 14,960 pairs of pantyhose to women customers at three games so far this season [1970]. "It's a conversation piece in Washington." It is indeed, particularly since the Washington *Post* head-lined: NATS LAST IN EAST, FIRST IN PANTYHOSE. Molomot's other inspirations get talked about, too: Camera Day, during which the teams line up on the field to be photographed by the fans and flash bulbs and film are given away; the monthly Lucky Fan Night, with a . . . [new] Camaro as the door prize; and the birthday parties at which a kid can see his name on the scoreboard and treat five friends to cake, all for $27.

None of this is calculated to soothe Washington's base-ball purists. Why, they want to know, is the team's $150,000 budget for promotion—plus salaries for a staff of five—not applied instead to reduction of the price of tickets? The game, they insist, will sell itself if the price is right and the team wins games.

"Helmet Night"

Molomot, a fifty-one-year-old bachelor who had gone to only two major-league games in his life before he was brought to the Senators by owner Bob Short, couldn't disagree more. Surveys, he says, show that the price of tickets has no rela-tion to attendance. And he argues that last season, the first year of the new promotion, attendance rose to 918,000, al-most double that of the preceding year. Of course, the new manager, Ted Williams, and the fact that the Senators pro-duced a respectable record had something to do with that. But so did the gimmicks, seemingly. "Take last week," said a Molomot aide. "The Senators had had a five-game losing streak on the road. They came home Tuesday and drew 14,927 people. Those people didn't come out to see the team. They came out because of Helmet Night (i.e., plastic bat-ting helmets were handed out)."

Or take last year, when the season was as good as over and the Senators had failed in an attempt to take over third place. "The next night," said the aide, "17,800 people turned out. Why? Because it was Hawaii Night. They got fresh pineapple and a chance on a free trip to Hawaii."

The Senators, of course, are by no means the only major-league team to indulge in gimmicks and giveaways. Cincinnati, for instance, has a "Grade A Day" to which children bring their report cards for admission, and the St. Louis Cardinals offer rain bonnets for the ladies ("I call that negative promotion," says Molomot). But the Washington team's PR staff insists that the Senators get at least twice as much promotion as any other team in either league. And though diehard fans may think that's much too much, Molomot expects this year's attendance to reach a break-even point of 1.2 million, in contrast to last year's over-all loss of $600,000. "I'm like a lost soul in a colony of purists," Molomot complains. "They believe baseball should sustain itself. But you've got to merchandise a good product. You've got to tell people."

WINNING IS A MANY SPLENDORED THING [5]

Baltimore, long famed as a port, as an industrial center, and as the locale where Francis Scott Key wrote the words for the "Star Spangled Banner," has been billing itself as The City of Champions.

It can boast of 1970 world champs in professional baseball and football and divisional champs in basketball and hockey.

Its teams are no slouches this year [1971] either. The one team whose season is over, the baseball Orioles, didn't quite reach its exalted 1970 level, but *did* win the American League pennant before losing the World Series to the Pittsburgh Pirates. And the football Colts, basketball Bullets and hockey Clippers are all strong.

[5] Article in *Nation's Business*. 59:70-2. D. '71. © 1971, *Nation's Business*—the Chamber of Commerce of the United States. Reprinted by permission.

What does having championship teams do for a city?

"It's realistic to say that everyone benefits—merchants, fans, government, and, through the psychological uplift of being number one, the city as a whole," says Baltimore's retiring Mayor Thomas J. D'Alesandro III.

In terms of hard cash, it's estimated that professional sports have been generating some $20 million in direct spending in Baltimore yearly. Post-season games—the World Series and playoffs—have generated an estimated $5 million more.

Experts say there is a multiplier effect as such spending circulates through a city's economy. In Baltimore's case, one economist says, he would use a multiplier of three. This would indicate a total spending figure of $60 million for regular-season games and $15 million for post-season contests, or a grand total of some $75 million.

That may not loom terribly large for a metropolitan area whose population tops two million (city population: 905,000). But much of it might not have been spent in Baltimore if the teams weren't there. It's frosting on the metropolitan cake.

And its value in terms of such intangibles as community spirit, and publicity that helps attract industry and trade, are potentially of greater importance, says Edward J. McNeal, executive vice president of Baltimore's Retail Merchants Association and executive director of the Committee for Downtown, Inc.

Everyone Likes a Winner

This is illustrated by the story of the Baltimore businessman who, at a gathering in another city, met the president of a large insurance firm that was thinking of moving its headquarters.

"What do you know about Baltimore?" he asked.

"Oh, I know Baltimore," the company president replied. "You've got the Orioles and the Colts."

The amount of nationwide publicity for pro teams these days is sky high. For championship teams, it's astronomical.

"Everybody likes a winner, and people around the country have the impression that Baltimore is a winner," says William Boucher III, executive director of the Greater Baltimore Committee. At home, he says, the teams' success has contributed to a sense of unity—something "a city searches for desperately these days."

Herbert G. Bailey, Jr., executive vice president of the Baltimore Chamber of Commerce, says that because of the games' wide appeal, they can help start dialogues between those of different races and economic levels.

Successful teams are particularly appealing to the local fans and to others from out of town who bring new money into the economy. Baltimore's Convention and Visitors Council sells the Orioles, Bullets and Clippers as attractions to potential conventioneers and other visitors. (There is not much point in doing so with the Colts. Like many pro football teams with hordes of season-ticket holders, the Colts are sold out.)

Measuring the economic effect of pro sports on a city is at best inexact. However, Dr. William A. Schaffer, a Georgia Tech economist and faculty member, thinks studies by Tech's Industrial Management Center are somewhere in the ball park. Dr. Schaffer headed surveys of the impact of the Atlanta Braves baseball team in 1966, the Atlanta Falcons football team in 1967 and the Montreal Expo baseball club in 1969.

Interviewers asked fans in the stands how much they were spending on tickets, food and entertainment, on concessions, transportation and lodgings. Club owners provided information, as did trade associations, individual businesses and municipal agencies. Among the salient facts: Taking the multiplier factor into account, baseball and football had a yearly over-all spending impact on Atlanta of $46 million, and in Montreal, baseball's impact was $25 million. And man for man, out-of-towners were the big spenders.

Similar studies have not been conducted in Baltimore, but Orioles Vice President Joseph P. Hamper, Jr., estimates about 30 percent of the baseball fans come from outside metropolitan Baltimore. The Colts estimate up to 5 percent of their season-ticket holders are from outside the area. And Bullets Executive Vice President Jerry Sachs says a recent survey indicates 30 percent of basketball fans are outsiders.

Robert England, director of sales at the Lord Baltimore Hotel, says sports events are steady contributors to occupancy rates during regular seasons, and their impact has been tremendous during playoffs and the World Series.

"Our occupancy rate more than doubles at Series time," he says. "The bars do three times their normal business, and restaurants are jammed. We have to add about 20 percent to our staff."

Mayor D'Alesandro says each Series game brings some $250,000 in new money to this city. And "these dollars turn over in goods, services and employment in the community," he says.

One by-product of pro sports involves the players more than the fans. Many players live year-round in the Baltimore area, and superstars' high salaries add to the economy both in consumption and investment. The Colts' Johnny Unitas owns a Baltimore restaurant. The Orioles' Brooks Robinson has a sporting-goods store.

Sports also have been good business for the city treasury, according to Douglas Tawney, Baltimore's director of parks and recreation. A hike in the state amusement tax pulled city-owned Memorial Stadium out of the red for the first time . . . [in 1970]. The city retains a slice of the tax amounting to over $500,000 annually from tickets to Colts and Orioles games. To this must be added some $800,000 in rental and concessions revenues.

Spreading the Profits

At the Civic Center, Executive Director Harold J. Jennifer, Jr., runs a precision operation that can convert a large auditorium into a basketball court or hockey rink in hours. It sometimes does both on the same day.

Together, the Bullets and Clippers had a 25 percent increase in total attendance in 1970. Fans who watched the Bullets win the Eastern Division title and lose the National Basketball Association playoff brought approximately $266,000 to the Center from taxes, rental and concessions. The Clippers are estimated to have contributed $185,000 in revenues.

Both the Orioles and Colts were profitable in 1970. Without the proceeds from the World Series, though, the Orioles would have posted a loss instead of a profit of $345,000. . . .

Although the Colt franchise is privately held, management furnished *Nation's Business* an income statement that showed a profit of $119,400 for the 1970 season, which ended when the Colts defeated the Dallas Cowboys in the Superbowl. At home, the Colts played to 420,000 fans during the regular season and 107,000 during playoffs.

Among the best evidence of what championship status means is that offered by Philip "Pinny" Friedman, owner of downtown Baltimore's Chesapeake Restaurant. Mr. Friedman began running a chartered bus service to Colts games from his restaurant in 1948. In those days, when the Colts were not at the top of the heap and "weren't drawing flies," he says, he was sometimes the only passenger. Nowadays, he says three hundred or more fans are transported—just about the number of diners he can serve in his restaurant.

CORRUPTING THE AMATEURS [6]

Every year the lads who are the flower of American high school athletics are besieged by college representatives osten-

[6] From "Playing the Game: Sports-Crazy Colleges Continue to Lure Stars With Improper Offers," by David DuPree, staff reporter. *Wall Street Journal.* p 1+. O. 8, '70. Reprinted by permission.

sibly bent on building character—alumni, coaches and others who try to convince prospects that four years of old Armageddon Tech forges manhood out of callow youth.

If the fullback who can run through a brick wall won't buy that, there are other, whispered promises. After awhile, the athlete announces to a waiting world that he has indeed chosen Armageddon Tech, saying it offered him the best chance to develop his hidden personal potential. Then he roars off in his new red Ferrari to inspect his new apartment and wardrobe.

Warren Brown, assistant executive director of the National Collegiate Athletic Association, the ruling body in college sport, says that fewer such irregularities in recruiting now come to the NCAA's attention. Observers note that the NCAA generally waits for formal complaints before investigating alleged violations—and they maintain that the only reason the organization isn't up to its eyeballs in complaints is that almost all those who would cast the first stone now live in glass houses themselves.

As Bad as Ever

Says one former coach in the Pacific Eight Conference: "It's kinda hard to try to hang another guy for the same crime you're committing." His comments are supported by talks with high school athletes, coaching personnel and others who indicate that improper recruiting, far from being on the decline, is as bad as ever and maybe worse.

Under NCAA rules, the most a college can offer an athlete is a summer job and a scholarship covering room, board and tuition. But the pressure to field winners in the major sports like football and basketball, which produce big gate and TV revenues and keep alumni purse strings loosened, is too great. "There are so few really good prospects every year," says one coach in the football-mad Southeastern Conference, "an.. you have to get your share of them or you don't stay a coach very long."

The result is an apparent gentlemen's agreement in which schools don't make trouble for one another with the NCAA—so long as no one gets too greedy—while continuing to offer lavish extras to the prospects. It's much the same as it was eighteen years ago, when running-back Hugh McElhenny, leaving the University of Washington to join the San Francisco '49ers, said he wasn't sure he could afford the cut in salary. (Asked how he chose Washington in the first place, McElhenny said: "I followed a trail of twenties.")

The bidding for the top prospects has become so fierce that some young athletes are getting disgusted. Jim McAlister is one. As a senior running-back at Blair High School in Pasadena, California, he gained 2,168 yards and scored thirty-one touchdowns last season [1969], a near-incredible performance that earned him a place on the High School All-America team—and made him the recruiting target of some sixty schools.

He finally chose the University of California at Los Angeles, a decision that prompted one disappointed bidder-coach to say: "UCLA really did a job on that boy. Must have offered him half of Hollywood." As a matter of fact, Jim says he picked UCLA precisely because it offered him no more than the rules allow.

Almost all the others, he says, tried to bribe him with lavish and illegal fringe benefits, or promised things Jim didn't believe they could deliver. "They tried to buy me," he says with distaste. "When I told them I didn't want any of that stuff, they started canceling trips they had planned for me to visit their campuses. UCLA just treated me as a person. That may sound simple but it's more than the others did."

An Athlete's Charges

An outstanding athlete who requests anonymity because he fears reprisals for "rocking the boat" claims that the University of Arizona offered him a Chevrolet Stingray convertible; the University of Colorado found a ranch-style home it was willing to rent him for $25 a month, and Columbia University offered a degree, "no matter what" his actual scholastic aptitude turned out to be. Other schools, he asserts, mentioned unlimited use of credit cards, trips home whenever needed and toll-free long-distance phone service, and one even proposed a scholarship for the athlete's non-athletic brother. Alabama topped all by simply saying "You name it and you've got it," he claims.

All the schools mentioned categorically deny any charges of offering illegal inducements to athletes. Frank Soltys, director of sports information at the University of Arizona, sums up their opinions when he says that "any shady deals one hears about you can boil down to braggadocio on the part of the athlete in question."

The athlete who maintains he got improper offers from Arizona and elsewhere says they were firm and serious proposals, some made by members of coaching staffs and others by alumni, who often serve as negotiators in such matters. (Many schools, however, frown on the extensive use of old grads because they are apt to make offers that violate the rules. "We don't use them too often," says football coach John McKay at the University of Southern California. "They just don't know the rules; something always seems to get lost in the translation.")

Criticism of improper recruiting is beginning to mount within the athletic fraternity itself. John McKenna, a former Virginia Military Institute coach who now is assistant athletic director at Georgia Tech, says he will never return to coaching because of the "fawning on teenaged athletes" that the job often requires.

Bill Bradley, the Princeton basketball star who now is a member of the champion New York Knicks, says: "The recruitment process, with the scholarships, the letters of intent (tentative agreements between prospect and school), is organized as a means for adult men to manipulate eighteen-year-olds, to get them to come to a university and provide it with a winning team, with money, with fame."

A high school coach in California recently resigned as an assistant coach at a big Western university because, he says, the intensity of the recruiting and the heavy payoffs involved sickened him. "There isn't one thing a big-time coach can't do for a boy if he wants to," he declares. "That includes money, cars and women."

Getting Caught

Now and then, of course, somebody gets caught. Texas A&M, the University of Minnesota, Marshall University and the University of North Carolina are currently being punished by the NCAA for recruiting violations. And punishment can be costly indeed.

The University of Houston, for example, drew a three-year probation, with sanctions, in 1966 for various football recruiting violations. This meant the school was ineligible for any post-season bowl games and forbidden to perform on television for three years. School officials estimate the penalty cost them at least $500,000.

In 1967, the year after Houston was nailed, the University of Illinois was accused of operating a slush fund—a kitty from which money is doled out to athletes. When the fund was exposed by a disgruntled assistant coach, all the coaches involved, as well as the athletic director, were forced to resign. The school was put on probation, and fourteen athletes were declared ineligible.

The Illinois coaches' defense was, in part, the argument that they were only doing what everyone else was doing. A coach at another Big Ten school agrees. "The only difference between Illinois and a lot of other schools is that Illinois got caught," he concedes.

The coaches who do a good deal of recruiting point out that they have more nettlesome problems than just deciding whether to offer that seven-foot center a convertible or a hardtop. One headache is the athlete who is way below par academically. One coach tells of a track man, barely literate after snoring his way through high school, who pondered what to put in the space marked "race or nationality" on his college admissions application. Finally he scrawled: "The 440-yard dash."

If the high school athlete is just too poor academically to be admitted, the coaching staff may arrange to salt him away temporarily at another, smaller school, usually with relaxed standards, from which he can transfer later. One prominent coach says he has yet to see a school lose a boy it really wanted because of poor grades. "If they want him badly enough, they'll get him," he declares. "They'll stick him in a junior college first or something, but they'll get him."

Another problem is the high school flash who all but demands a promise of first-string status in college. "Many kids want a guarantee that they'll play no matter what," says USC's John McKay. "You can't give that to a kid. All you can offer is a scholarship and a fair chance."

A long courtship also helps, too, giving school and prospect a chance to get to know and appreciate each other. Jim McAlister of UCLA, for example, was first approached by that school in the summer after his sophomore year at Blair High. From the start, UCLA sensed that things other than football were important to their young prospect.

"They prepared me for college two years ahead of time," recalls Jim. "They told me what courses I needed to take and all the other things I needed to know to get ready for college. But the important thing was they never lied to me or promised me things they had no business promising."

At first, being wooed was fun, he admits. But then the constant effort by the recruiters to top each other's bids, the escalating, illegal offers, got to Jim. He also noticed that "a lot of them weren't too anxious to tell me what I wanted to know about the school itself, as if they were hiding something."

Jim's coach at Blair, Pete Yoder, quit after the 1969-70 season to take a job as an assistant coach at USC, which also was after Jim. To the young athlete this was just the Pied

Piper ploy—often used in recruiting—in which a young athlete can be induced to come to the school prudent enough
to find a job for his old coach. Mr. Yoder denies that was
the case; he says he had been considering his decision for a
couple of years, didn't take the USC job to influence Jim
and intends to stay there.

III. THE PROMOTERS

EDITOR'S INTRODUCTION

For most fans the word *promoter* conjures up images of cigar-chomping, middle-aged fight managers trying to wheel and deal their way into "the big time." The image is obsolescent. Today's sports promoter, if not a top-rated Ivy League lawyer or graduate of the Harvard School of Business Administration, is likely to be an elegantly clad vice president at one of the major TV networks. A new polish has entered the field, but the old objectives still seem to hold. Whether or not the practitioners sweat visibly, bringing home the bacon is still the ultimate goal.

This section is devoted to some of the ploys and foibles of the men who promote sports in America today. The first article, by Richard L. Worsnop, traces the history of pro sports' rise to affluence, marking out the role of such influential forces as television in the way the game is played. That professional sports have become highly dependent on television revenue, as described by Worsnop, is an indication of the kind of promotional influence sports are being subjected to. The next article, by a former defensive-back in the National Football League, Bernie Parrish, spells out in lurid detail precisely what television's promotional clout has done to the game. In Parrish's view, the massive revenues generated by commercial TV may, oddly, have whetted the owners' appetite for the prospective financial bonanzas inherent in pay TV, and thus cooked, to some extent, the goose that has been laying the golden egg.

The third article in this section, from *Newsweek,* reports on the famed Joe Frazier-Muhammad Ali heavyweight champion boxing match of 1971 and notes that "the promoters succeeded by keeping prices high and the audience limited.

Thus they effectively locked out the rank and file who keep sports alive with their support. . . . In catering to such a small and affluent minority, can sports promoters still hope for the indulgence of the public and the exemptions they now enjoy from the antitrust laws?"

The last article, by a former sports editor of the London *Observer*, shows that commercialism and the drive for profits are not solely the province of professional American athletics. In Britain too, it would seem, money is king when it comes to sports.

"SELFISH, CALLOUS AND UNGRATEFUL" [1]

Professional athletes have always been regarded by Americans with a mixture of admiration and condescension. Saturday's hero is likely to be viewed on Monday as just another "dumb jock." Leonard Shecter [journalist and author of books on sports] recalled:

Not long ago professionals were allowed to compete at fancy country clubs but were asked not to use the main entrance or hang around the clubhouse bar. Baseball players were counted ruffians and part-time bartenders (and indeed, they were often both). Professional football players, who came much later, were underpaid animals, fit for nothing but slamming each other around in the mud during poorly attended Sunday afternoon games.

Derision of the professional athlete appears deeply rooted in Anglo-Saxon tradition. An anonymous British author stated the case as long ago as August 13, 1870, in a magazine called *Every Saturday*:

Indeed, it may be doubted whether the modern system of cultivating athletes, namely by a fierce competition stimulated by heavy bribes, does not inflict positive moral injury, by developing animal intensity of the will—the root of one kind of cruelty—and a hungry greed for more money earned without toil. . . . Nobody is quite so 'hard' as the professional sporting man, quite so incapable of pity, remorse or self-restraint in the pursuit of gain.

[1] From "Professional Athletes," by Richard L. Worsnop, staff writer. *Editorial Research Reports.* v 2, no 9:679-86. S. 1, '71. Reprinted by permission.

Rise of Baseball

Professional team-sports had their beginning in the United States in 1869, the year the Cincinnati Red Stockings were founded. Two years later, the National Association of Professional Base Ball Players was formed, thus sounding the death knell for amateur or club baseball. An unprecedented sports boom soon followed. The years from 1875 to 1900 brought the first running of the Kentucky Derby, the Preakness, and the Belmont; the founding of the National (baseball) League; the first gloved championship boxing bout; the start of the sports page by William Randolph Hearst; opening of the first Madison Square Garden; and donation of the Davis Cup, the world tennis championship trophy.

Abuses of both amateur and professional sport were not long in appearing. Seven members of the 1893 football squad at the University of Michigan were not even students. "Yale lured James Hogan, a superb tackle, to New Haven at the turn of the century by giving him a suite in Vanderbilt Hall, free meals, a trip to Cuba, free tuition, a monopoly on the sale of scorecards, and the job as cigarette agent for the American Tobacco Company" (Robert H. Boyle. *Sport— Mirror of American Life.*).

In the early years of professional baseball, it was commonplace for players to bet on games—and they did not always wager on their own team. Another unsavory practice was "tipping"; in 1917 the Chicago White Sox collected $45 per man to "tip" the Detroit Tigers for beating the Boston Red Sox in an important series. "From 1917 through 1920," Shecter asserted, "there are so many records of bribery that one has to be suspicious of *all* games of that era."

Baseball's darkest hour came in 1919, when eight members of the Chicago White Sox conspired with gamblers to throw the World Series to the Cincinnati Reds. The "Black Sox scandal, which did not come to light until September 1920, aroused widespread revulsion and cynicism among baseball fans. To repair the damage, Judge Kenesaw Mountain Landis was appointed baseball's high commissioner on November 7, 1920, and given virtually autocratic powers. His first official act was to place all eight White Sox players involved in the scandal on baseball's ineligible list; after they were acquitted in court on conspiracy-to-defraud charges, the commissioner banned them from the game for life.

Baseball quickly recovered from the Black Sox affair and attained new peaks of popularity in the 1920s, still thought of as the game's golden age. The twenties, in fact, were a golden age for all professional sports. The public's athletic heroes included not only such baseball stars as Babe Ruth, Ty Cobb and Walter Johnson, but also tennis player William Tilden, golfer Bobby Jones, and football player Red Grange.

TV's Role in Popularity of Football, Basketball

Grange, a halfback for the University of Illinois, was instrumental in stirring interest in professional football. Joining the Chicago Bears immediately after his last college game, Grange proceeded to play in 10 pro games in only 16 days. The "Galloping Ghost" attracted capacity crowds, and within three months he and his manager had earned $100,000 each.

> This . . . made Grange the highest-paid player in the history of pro football [up till then], but of more importance to the [National Football] League was the fact of that, for the first time, pro football monopolized sports pages all over the nation. This was the first big impact the sport had on the American public and the interest created by Grange was never to die down again [writes author Tex Maule].

Professional football did not come into its own, however, until the advent of network television. At first, each National Football League team made its own television deal. Rights to New York Giants games brought $200,000, highest in the league; most other clubs had to settle for about $40,000 a year. Then, in 1960, the fledgling American Football League and the American Broadcasting Company signed the first league-network contract—a five-year, $1.6 million agreement. A year later, the NFL and the Columbia Broadcasting System followed suit with a two-year, $9.3 million pact.

A Federal district court judge declared the NFL-CBS contract to be in violation of the antitrust laws, thus forcing the league to return to team-by-team negotiation. Carrying the fight to Congress, the NFL lobbied for a bill legalizing single-network TV contracts with professional sports leagues. Legislation to this end was signed by President Kennedy on September 30, 1961; four months later, on January 10, 1962, the NFL and CBS signed a new two-year contract for the same amount as the old one.

Pro football's television revenue—apportioned equally among all teams—has climbed steadily since 1962; in the 1970 season, it came to more than $40 million, or more than one third of the $110 million total revenue of the twenty-six-team National Football League. Television also provided other professional sports leagues with substantial income. The twenty-four major-league baseball teams grossed around $160 million in 1970, including $38 million from sale of TV rights; the twenty-eight teams of the American and National Basketball associations grossed $40 million in the 1970-71 season, of which $9 million came from television; and the fourteen National Hockey League teams grossed $40 million, including $3 million in TV money.

Professional sports, in short, have become highly dependent on television revenue; without it, many teams might be forced to cease operation. As it is, only half of all major-league baseball teams broke even or made a profit last season. Pro teams have been forced to make minor alterations in the way games are played so as to accommodate television. For example, special timeouts for commercials are now called during football games. And the 1967 baseball All-Star game, held in Anaheim, California, began at the unusual hour of 4 P.M. Pacific Daylight Time so that it could be seen in prime television time in the East.

Television's role in sports is resented by numerous pro athletes. Bill Russell, former player-coach of the Boston Celtics, asserted:

> If you don't watch those TV people they will devour you. First they ask you to call timeouts so they can get in their commercials. Then they tell you *when* to take them. Then they want to get into the locker room at halftime. Then more and more and more. If you don't put on the brakes they'll tell you when to play.

Expansion and Mergers of Rival Leagues in 1960s

Television played a major role also in the shifting of franchises, creation of new teams, and mergers of rival leagues that took place in the 1960s. The move of the Milwaukee (formerly Boston) Braves to Atlanta in 1966 was motivated almost solely by the prospect of additional broadcast revenue. In Milwaukee, the Braves were hemmed in by the Chicago White Sox and Cubs to the south, the Minnesota Twins to the west, and the Detroit Tigers to the east. Atlanta, in contrast, offered virtually all of the South as a radio-TV market.

When the New York Giants and Brooklyn Dodgers of the National League moved to California before the start of the 1958 season, they set in motion a chain of events that three years later led to major-league baseball's first expansion in sixty years. The American League showed the way in 1961 by increasing its size from eight to ten teams. One new—"expansion"—team was placed in Los Angeles and the other in the nation's capital, to replace the old Washington Senators, who moved to the Twin Cities of Minneapolis-St. Paul and called themselves the Minnesota Twins.

In 1962 the National League followed suit and placed one expansion team in New York and one in Houston. "However, lucrative television revenues and the ever-growing popularity of the sport brought the desire for further expansion." This occurred in 1969, when both leagues expanded to twelve teams. The American League placed a team in Seattle and one in Kansas City, the latter taking the place of the Athletics, who had moved to Oakland [California] in 1968. The National League placed a team in San Diego and one in Montreal, which marked the first time a major-league baseball team was based outside the United States. The twelve-team leagues then established divisions consisting of six teams each.

Similar activity took place in other professional sports leagues. The twelve-team National Football League awarded a franchise to Dallas in 1960 and to Minneapolis-St. Paul in 1961. Further expansion occurred in 1968, when Atlanta was awarded a franchise, and in 1967, when New Orleans became the sixteenth NFL team. Meanwhile, the rival American Football League, which began operations in 1960, had survived its shaky beginnings and achieved financial health. The two leagues announced merger plans June 8, 1966, which by the 1970 season resulted in a twenty-six-team National Football League, divided into two conferences, National and American.

Professional basketball underwent many of the changes experienced by football in the 1960s. The established National Basketball Association added new teams and attracted more fans and broadcasting revenue. And like the NFL, it found itself faced with a rival—the American Basketball Association. The NBA initially ignored the ABA—as the NFL had done at first in the case of the AFL—but costly salary competition for players led both sides to explore the possibilities of a merger. Preliminary talks to that end were held in 1969 and 1970, but the NBA players succeeded in winning a temporary restraining order, April 17, 1970, suspending the negotiations. The NBA Players' Association has since vowed to fight any common player-draft arrangement that "restrains and restricts" a player's ability to use competitive bidding to win higher salaries. Legislation to authorize an ABA-NBA merger was introduced in the Senate on July 29, 1971. [The legislation failed, but a modified version of the bill was introduced in 1973.—Ed.]

In the absence of a merger, bidding between the ABA and NBA for playing talent has reached unprecedented heights. Johnny Neumann, a University of Mississippi sophomore, signed with the ABA's Memphis Pros for $2 million; Spencer Haywood jumped from the ABA's Denver Rockets to the NBA's Seattle SuperSonics for $1.5 million; and Howard Porter of Villanova, most valuable player in the 1971 National Collegiate Athletic Association basketball tournament, signed with the NBA's Chicago Bulls for $1.5 million. It was revealed in June 1971 that Porter had signed an agreement in December 1970 to play in the ABA Because the agreement violated NCAA rules, Villanova was forced to forfeit its second-place finish in the tournament.

Professional football's experience suggests that a merger, by eliminating competitive bidding, does indeed lower the bonus and salary offers made to draftees. "Without the stimulus of the AFL-NFL rivalry the prices for football talent have been dropping steadily," Morton Sharnik . . . reported in *Sports Illustrated.* "This year they've plummeted. Presumably, the clubs' offers reflect the state of the economy. However, there is good reason to believe that they also reflect a desire by the teams to discredit [players'] agents. . . ."

Proliferation of New Sports Stadiums and Arenas

The expansion of professional sports over the past ten years or so has been accompanied by a burst of construction of new stadiums and arenas. No fewer than 12 of the 24 major-league baseball teams play in stadiums that opened in 1961 or later, and pro football teams are co-tenants in most of them. The New England Patriots moved into a new stadium at Foxboro, Massachusetts, in mid-August. Additional stadiums are being built or are planned in Kansas City, northern New Jersey, New Orleans, and the Dallas, Detroit and Baltimore areas.

The new home of the Philadelphia Phillies—and in football season, the Eagles—provides their patrons with plush

seats, attractive female ushers in hot pants ("Super Fillies")
and a multi-million-dollar scoreboard. It flashes commercials
and, when a Phillie hits a home run, depicts the following
images, as described in the magazine *Philadelphia*: "two
giant dolls, a Liberty Bell, a cannon, a flag that rolls up by
itself, dancing waters and seven thousand Macedonians in
full battle array." The author commented further: "If Connie Mack Stadium had been in South Philadelphia, the
Phillies would still be playing there. . . ." Connie Mack
Stadium recently was gutted by fire. Meanwhile, at their
new home in Veterans Stadium, the Phillies have drawn
more than twice as many fans—1,133,359—in fifty-four home
dates than in all of 1970.

The New Orleans stadium project is the most ambitious
to date, and it has become an issue in the Louisiana gubernatorial race. Plans call for an 80,000-seat domed-stadium on
the order of the Astrodome in Houston. "If constructed it
will be one of the world's most capacious buildings, in a
league with St. Peter's Basilica and the Pentagon" [according
to an article in *Sports Illustrated*, June 7, 1971]. The project
is controversial because its projected cost, estimated at
$35 million in 1966, has since climbed to $129.5 million. A
stadium built for that amount of money, it is calculated,
would have to take in $35,000 a day in rental revenue merely
to break even. [Construction was started in August 1971.
The stadium opened for the 1973 baseball season.—Ed.]

Stadium plans in other areas likewise have run into opposition. New York fans, including Mayor John V. Lindsay,
are upset that the pro football Giants signed a thirty-year
contract with New Jersey authorities to play, beginning in
1975, in a 75,000-seat stadium being planned as part of a
$200 million sports complex on swampland near East Ruther-
ford, New Jersey. New Yorkers fear that the other tenant of
Yankee Stadium, the namesake New York Yankees, might
follow the Giants to New Jersey. [The Yankees have since
decided to stay in New York.—Ed.] Lindsay, calling the
Giants' management "selfish, callous and ungrateful," said

he had asked [former] Representative Emanuel Celler of Brooklyn [Democrat, New York], chairman of the House Judiciary Committee [until January 1973], "to conduct an inquiry into this matter."

TV TUNES IN [2]

Nineteen sixty-four was the year the game changed. CBS president James Aubrey, "The Smiling Cobra," decided pro football was the coming thing for TV. CBS decided Aubrey wasn't and canned him in 1965. By then, however, our dressing rooms were aflood with show-biz types. Long hair, dark glasses, large gold cufflinks, and dress shirts with ruffles down the front accompanied "Fabulous, sweetie," and "Beautiful, baby, set the camera up over here," into the sanctuary of our locker rooms. Large black cables lay around the floors; there were cameras and hot spotlights in the corners. . . .

Players complained about the intrusion of TV technical crews and the pompous interviews demanded by the pseudo-experts in the crested sports coats. When CBS executives paid $14.1 million to televise the NFL [National Football League] games, they acted as if they had bought the sport, including the people who played it. . . .

Some players prove as calculating as the ad men and TV directors. Dick Schafrath runs to shake the hand of any Browns player who scores a touchdown. He usually gets to the man in the end zone. The TV camera always follows the ballcarrier through the end zone as he scores and stays on him until he starts back toward his team's bench, and invariably, whenever the Browns score a touchdown, the TV announcer ends up saying, "And there's Dick Schafrath congratulating . . ." Exposure is valuable for Dick, who has had his eye on a movie career for as long as I have known him.

[2] From *They Call It a Game*, by Bernie Parrish, a former defensive-back in the National Football League. Dial. '71. Chapter 8 from *They Call It a Game*, by Bernie Parrish. Copyright © 1971 by Bernard P. Parrish. Reprinted by permission of the publisher, The Dial Press.

Bob Gain, a defensive-tackle for the Browns (1952-63), used to lie on the ground after a tackle until the PA system said his name. More than once we nearly started the next play before Bob got up. Sam Huff piled on a lot, and got away with it because of his press buildup. After a while it was dollars and cents TV exposure: "Also in on the tackle, number 70, Sam Huff." ...

"Circus for the Hordes"

When the camera's little red light goes on, we players put on our affected TV faces, too. Announcers we just met two minutes earlier we call by first names, as if we were old friends, catering to the medium like everyone else.

The field is even decorated differently with club emblems and colorful end-zone designs; brighter, more appealing packaging of the product is what the ad men call it—television technique.

The combination of the two most glamorous industries in the world, television and pro football, has produced an alliance with staggeringly powerful influence. [Former] Congressman Emanuel Celler [Democrat, New York] said, "Pro football provides the circus for the hordes." And, of course, it is presented through television. Madison Avenue advertising agencies are exploiting the game to the fullest. Their hidden persuaders are selling everything from cars to canned beef stew endorsed with the NFL emblem.

The explosion of TV income began January 24, 1964, and the drama of it all was described in purple prose by William Johnson in a series on sports and television for *Sports Illustrated*. Bill MacPhail, CBS vice president of sports, "with perhaps a trace of a catch in his voice," described copping the high bid of $28.2 million ($14.1 million per season for the 1964 and 1965 NFL regular seasons) as "my greatest moment in sport."

Johnson did an exhaustive study of circumstances and events that surrounded MacPhail's "moment" and wrote,

All the elements that make up the glamorous, scintillating, demanding, and unnerving world of network television came into play on this celebrated occasion—suspense, one-upmanship, avarice, jealousy, skulduggery, espionage, mendacity, conspicuous consumption. . . .

NBC's vice president of sports, Carl Lindemann, knew before he left his office for the opening of the supposedly secret bids that his was going to be too low; and before night fell he had NBC President Bob Kintner's approval to pay the rival American Football League a lifegiving $42 million for five years of telecast rights. The deal was completed four days later and ABC, which had gotten the AFL started, was out of pro football on its ear because a trusted employee either opposed the exorbitant costs and wanted ABC out of pro football or, as the rumors had it, accepted a $50,000 bribe to leak the amount of the ABC bid. CBS made a large, last-minute adjustment upwards to $14.1 million even though a smaller figure proposed by Jim Aubrey the day before had been assailed by William S. Paley, CBS board chairman, as a "money-be-damned approach, more irresponsible than Hollywood ever saw in its worst days."

On January 23, 1964, eleventh-hour maneuvering was going on as far away as Baltimore, where [Commissioner Pete] Rozelle's old sponsor, Carroll Rosenbloom, bought out his partners in the Baltimore Colts to become the sole . . . [beneficiary] of the "surprisingly" large increase in TV income guaranteed to the Colts by the new CBS contract.

$200,000 a Minute

Nineteen sixty-four was a year when [Coach Vince] Lombardi's Packers and [Johnny] Unitas's Colts were struggling for supremacy in the Western Conference while Jim Brown, doing his thing, was helping us destroy the New York Giant myth and a great old pro named Y. A. Tittle. These bitter rivalries gave fan interest the momentum that eventually drove the network rate to advertisers to more than $200,000 a minute for the 1970 Superbowl. An advertiser now pays upwards of $70,000 for each of eighteen to nineteen minutes of advertising time allotted to regular-season games. The price per minute is based on $7 to $8 per thousand households reached; and as John Delorean, general manager of the Chevrolet Division of General Motors says, "You know you're not reaching Maudie Frickert; you're reaching men, the guys who are making the decision to buy a car. Another major factor is that most of our dealers are sports fans. We feel it is almost as important to get our message to them as to our customers." Delorean is also a part owner of the San Diego Chargers.

Based on $7.50 per thousand, the network grossed approximately $84 million for the year. Chrysler Corporation alone spent more than $13 million to sell their cars to pro football's selective audience of eighteen-to-forty-nine-age-group males in the wholesome setting provided by football.

In 1956 the owners' income from TV and radio combined totaled $1,719,693 for twelve clubs, or an average of $143,307 per club. The average player's salary was $9,216. Today, in 1971, television and radio income has multipled itself 27 times over, to $49.35 million for the league or an average of about $1.9 million per club, 13 times more than in 1956, while players' salaries have increased less than 3 times over.

Rozelle and the owners are constantly plotting new ways to extract more dollars from television. Roone Arledge, president of ABC Sports, said, "Most of what TV does wrong is done to generate more dollars for owners. If we cram eighteen commercials into a football game it's because the owners and the leagues are so damned greedy in what they ask for rights."

When NBC saved the American Football League in 1964, it brought the merger of the two leagues within the realm of feasibility. But before it could become practical and profitable, television had to impose some changes on the game. The race of the also-rans at the end of the season had to be made more exciting to attract sponsors. Breaking the teams into smaller divisions of four and five teams each was just the gimmick. This would fix the competition so that no team would finish worse than fifth—fourth in most divisions —thereby increasing the chances for more exciting divisional races and making a playoff system necessary. This meant more games and, therefore, more television revenue.

What's Good for TV ...

In a sense, the Pro-Bowl game is "fixed" to be more exciting in the same way as is the divisional setup. Both John Brodie and John Hadl, quarterbacks for the Western Division Pro-Bowl and All-Star teams for the NFL and AFL in 1970, came up complaining to the referees after a linebacker blitzed on a pass play. Blitzing [rushing the quarterback to prevent a pass] was ruled out of the old NFL Pro-Bowl and AFL All-Star games by prearrangement. There was no blitzing in the 1971 American Football Conference-National Football Conference All-Star game either, so the same rule is still in effect. The reasoning given is that it is too difficult for the offensive linemen to iron out their terminology and methods of blocking the blitzers in the short amount of time the players from different teams have to prepare for the games. Limiting the defensive strategy cuts down on the quarterbacks' and receivers' recognition problems and makes it easier for the offense to predict what defense they will be facing when they start each play. This makes for a higher-scoring, more exciting television program. It is a contrived TV script. Because of this, I refused to play in the Pro Bowl in January 1965.

Realignment into two conferences kept the AFL-NFL rivalry alive and also maximized fan interest. Switching Cleveland, Baltimore, and Pittsburgh from the NFL into the AFC not only balanced the number of teams in the

American Football Conference [AFC] and the National
Football Conference [NFC] with thirteen teams each, but it
also balanced up TV market areas, an important factor in
determining which teams would switch from the NFC to the
less prestigious AFC. The battle over realignment was fero-
cious. At one Palm Springs meeting it featured the then
president of the league, Arthur Modell, exchanging ethnic
insults with old crony Carroll Rosenbloom. Modell later
said, "It would emasculate the NFL for the Browns to switch
to the AFL." Then it was decided that each of the thirteen
NFC clubs remaining after realignment would pay $138,400
per year for five years to the clubs that switched—a total of
$2,998,666 for each of the three teams switching to the AFC.
Both Modell and Rosenbloom changed their tune and along
with "nice guy" Art Rooney, of the Pittsburgh Steelers, decided to take the money and switch. The Browns 1970 press
book records Modell's sudden change of heart this way:

> Modell is an innovator and no better example of his forward-
> thinking can be cited than his startling offer in the spring of 1969
> to move the Browns over to what had been the American Football
> League side of the fence.

The $3 million helped ease the blow to the old NFLers
switching leagues, and the [New York] Jets [AFL] victory
over the [Baltimore] Colts [NFL] in the 1969 Superbowl
was soothing too.

Without the victory of the underdog New York Jets in
January 1969, the merger could well have been a monstrous
disaster for CBS and NBC. Some of the staunchest NFL
fans, particularly those in Cleveland and Baltimore, were up
in arms over their teams having to go into that *other* league.
But after the Jets' upset, things quieted down and a new
feeling of wait-until-next-year began to well up in Baltimore,
where the Colts would end up, conveniently, being in the
same division with "that damn Joe Namath" [of the Jets]—
a chance for revenge.

Squeezing Out the Last Buck

Namath and his teammates' performance secured the two leagues at the very least $100 million in future TV revenue. The game was almost too good to be true. Considering other devices imposed by TV's needs to lift fan interest and raise the advertisers' prices, perhaps it *was* too good to be true. What troubles me is that TV looks at the game pragmatically as an infinite number of unique program scripts. A Colt slaughter of the Jets would have confirmed the public's suspicions of a gross imbalance between the two leagues. The Kansas City Chiefs' opportune win in 1970 all but wiped out that suspicion.

Dick Bailey, president of the Hughes Sports Network, said, "No one I know can squeeze the last buck out of a situation the way Pete Rozelle can"—a lesson the players have learned the hard way.

Rozelle urged George Halas to move his Bears out of Wrigley Field in Chicago to Soldier Field, a stadium with lights, so regular-season games could eventually play to a sudden-death conclusion. Sudden death is a better way to decide which team goes to the playoffs than flipping a coin, and it will increase the number of commercials in the four to six games that usually end in ties each season. Sudden-death playoffs will be harder on the players, as are the ABC-TV Monday night games. The players can live with both of them, but they should be compensated for the additional hardships.

The television networks claim they are caught in a squeeze. Their affiliates, the local stations, demand pro football games, and the league presses for more money. The industry experts say they must have the prestige of pro football to satisfy the affiliates, and the sponsors are screaming about the price. At the same time, television's executives, like Bill MacPhail, make like NFL owners and say their networks "do sports as a public service" because they don't make any profit from it.

When the league beckons, the networks respond because if they don't Howard Hughes is waiting, checkbook in hand. Control over the networks extends to approval of sportscasters by Rozelle himself. This provision reduces the men at the mikes to pitchmen impartial to everything but the league office and the owners, and whatever they're promoting at the moment. Thus television serves as the pulpit from which the throng are told that the draft, the option clause, the owners, and the high cost of tickets are part of an unalterable scripture brought down from the Mount on a stone tablet by Pete Rozelle.

Although it has been carefully denied, a blueprint for implementing pay-TV was drawn up by the league long ago. One of [former] Congressman Emanuel Celler's main objections to passing the merger bill was his not being told all the facts about the owners' future arrangements. Ralph Wilson, owner of the Buffalo Bills, predicted in an owners' merger-committee meeting July 21, 1966, that "carrying the game only on closed-circuit television could mean $25 million to $30 million in revenue." In 1964 Bud Adams predicted that in 1974 the sixteen old NFL clubs would be carving up $60 million a year. . . . Adams was wild-eyed about the prospects for pay TV. "We can send the games to England via Telstar. Send them anywhere! Europe! South America! We can create fans and they'll pay to watch." Arthur Modell's words of caution had fallen on deaf ears when he said a few weeks earlier, "You can't look greedy." But then he got a little carried away himself telling *Fortune* magazine, "I envision the time when the league will be the exhibitor, the operator, the promoter. We'll hire banquet halls and meeting rooms for screening the games ourselves."

$400 Million from Pay-TV?

The San Diego Chargers owner Eugene Klein has been using closed-circuit TV successfully for home games with arch-rival Oakland Raiders for several years. He is also president of National General Corporation which, among other

properties, owns Theater Color Television Corporation,
formed for the purpose of developing a nationwide closed-
circuit color-television network for theaters. Jack Kent Cook,
an owner of the Washington Redskins, was the man who
paid Joe Frazier and Muhammad Ali $2.5 million each to
carry their title fight in March of 1971 on closed-circuit television. [See "Big-Screen Promotions," in this section, below.]
The fight grossed $20 million and has the other NFL owners
licking their chops thinking about charging $10 a ticket
for closed-circuit televising of the 1974 Superbowl. If ten
million watched the game in their local banquet halls, meeting rooms, and theaters it would bring in $100 million.
Or there is the alternative plan to utilize CATV (cable television) which is the one that Rozelle himself pushes when
discussing the future of the league. A charge of $2 per set
for the Superbowl game would have brought in about
$70 million for 1970's extravaganza. And applying suitable
multiples, the regular season would have added another
$400 million. Franchise values will skyrocket proportionately
to $40 million or $50 million each. . . .

The words we hear coming from our television sets don't
seem to have the same meaning as they used to, whether
they are coming from the White House or the NFL hucksters.
The images we see are what the paid packagers want us to
see. In the case of pro football the packages are designed and
decorated behind the closed doors of the commissioner's office, and there is no consumer protection for the public.

Using television and the other media, owners tell the
public their profit has been eaten up by inflationary costs.
But it isn't true. The owners have chosen to consume their
huge television income on organizational power before their
bookkeepers get to the line marked net profit. The clubs
have built expensive top-heavy corporations that are designed to emphasize and protect the owners' phoney importance to the game. The league office has led the way buying
influence with the people they hire. One owner readily ad-

mitted to *TV Guide* that administrative costs had risen 45 percent faster than players' salaries, while scouting-system costs have blown up 2000 percent more than players' salaries since 1953. Television income has gone from $1,239,149 (for TV *and* radio) in 1953 to over $46.5 million for 1971, a whopping increase of 3900 percent. With gate receipts bringing in over $100 million, more than enough to pay *necessary* expenses, the TV income could be taken a clear profit if the owners chose to take it. Instead, they use it up on their huge perpetuating machine of public-relations employees operating under various titles in club front-offices and scouting systems. These large intricate organizations tend to institutionalize and insulate owners from the players and public they are bilking. But of course the Government would get half the TV money in taxes if the owners didn't invest it in depreciating computers, front offices overstaffed with patronizing employees, and other amusements.

BIG-SCREEN PROMOTIONS [3]

When Joe Frazier floored Muhammad Ali with a left hook in the fifteenth round, some 1,500 spectators at the Forum in Inglewood, California, were watching him throw a right. The viewers were not imagining things; they had simply purchased $10 bargain seats behind the huge closed-circuit television screen, and they had to watch the images dance across the screen in reverse. If they had wanted to see the fight head-on, they could have bought tickets earlier and paid $25. For in the world of closed-circuit promotion, the general rule is first come, first served—and bring money.

The Forum is owned by Jack Kent Cooke, who put up most of the fighters' purse-money and co-promoted the event with theatrical agent Jerry Perenchio. Since Cooke and Perenchio anticipated a $2.5 million profit out of the $25 million gross gate, Cooke hardly needed to cram those

[3] From "Greed Creed: Will It Pay Off?" *Newsweek*. 77:75D-6. Mr. 22, '71. Copyright Newsweek, Inc. 1971, reprinted by permission.

few extra bodies behind his screen. But the gesture added a fitting Alice-in-Wonderland touch to the colorful worldwide happening; and it also emphasized the one element that seemed constant wherever the show went on—the spirit of greed. If the action in the ring stirred a wide range of emotions in those who watched, the action outside it provoked considerable anger and some hard new looks at the entire closed-circuit phenomenon.

At the Chicago Coliseum, an equipment failure—the nightmare of all closed-circuit exhibitors—sent thousands into an angry riot that was finally ended with blasts from fire hoses. In Cooke's Forum, even the fans in front of the screen complained bitterly about the disgracefully murky color picture. And across the country, lawyers began grappling with the suits that have been filed by local promoters who were not cut in on the bonanza. But the deeper questions raised by the fight extended beyond such explosions and disputes. Is closed-circuit promotion the wave of the future in sports, as its proponents claim? And if so, what will it do to the social and legal bases on which sports stand?

For the most part, American sports have flourished because of their mass appeal. As long as they were being entertained and perhaps lifted momentarily above their daily routines, US sports fans tolerated the city-hopping of baseball owners, local blackouts of pro football games and countless other self-serving maneuvers by team owners and promoters. The courts took the same lenient position, allowing sports executives to use monopolistic practices that would never be condoned in normal business. If players had to sacrifice some individual rights and if fans had to miss a few games, it was presumably in the interest of a greater good—the assurance of top-grade entertainment for the millions.

Locking Out the Rank and File

Last week's fight seriously altered this equation: the promoters succeeded by keeping prices high and the audience limited. Thus they effectively locked out the rank and file who keep sports alive with their support but cannot pay $10 and up for tickets. There was disturbing irony in the fact that the estimated audiences for delayed home-television broadcasts in Italy and Japan outnumbered the viewers who saw the first landing on the moon—while the American audience was held down by price and theater capacity to a relatively scant 1.5 million people. In catering to such a small and affluent minority, can sports promoters still hope for the indulgence of the public and the exemptions they now enjoy from the antitrust laws?

New York *Times* columnist James Reston had perhaps the strongest answer:

> One argument for professional sport in America is that it occasionally diverts the whole nation from its normal preoccupations and provides the people with a common interest for at least a few hours. The closed-circuit system threatens to change all that: it is sport for the rich, like polo and yacht racing, with the poor outside the gate. . . . The possibilities of fair legislation to avoid the repetition or spread of the practice are fairly obvious.

Indeed, New Jersey Congressman Charles W. Sandman, Jr., . . . [in March 1971] introduced a bill that would give the Federal Communications Commission the power to issue permits and thus govern the previously uncontrolled closed-circuit promoters; it would also require such promoters to prove that public broadcasters had been given a chance to bid on events that wind up on closed circuit. The effect of Sandman's law might be minimal, since no network could approach the kind of bid Cooke and Perenchio made to get this fight. But such legislation might at least make promoters conscious of some answerability to the public, and it could also be a step toward modifying the iron-clad exclusivity that Perenchio demanded. One wonders, for instance, if the FCC would grant a promoter the unrestricted right to keep a fight off not only live home-television, but also off radio and delayed-news shows—as Cooke and Perenchio were able to do.

Actually, the fight promoters brought much of the reaction on themselves with their brazen flaunting of power.
Cooke and Perenchio even challenged the right of the press
to report the news; they went to court to seek to prevent the
wire services from transmitting round-by-round accounts of
the fight to broadcasters and newspapers for use while the
fight was still on. The attempt not only failed, but it turned
many newsmen against the closed-circuit concept.

The public, for the most part, seemed far less troubled
by the fight promotion. Radio stations in several areas did
take calls from angry fans who couldn't get tickets, and disgruntled crowds gathered outside filled arenas in some large
cities. But there was no groundswell of resentment, possibly
because few observers believe that the fight was more than a
one-shot phenomenon. It is inconceivable, for example, that
pro football, which owes its prosperity to network television,
would betray its fans for a quick closed-circuit profit on the
Superbowl; even less enlightened owners in sports like baseball and basketball seem equally certain to resist such temp-
tation. Thus, boxing may be the only sport suited to such
profiteering, because unlike regularly scheduled team-sports,
it doesn't have to depend on loyal attendance by steady, day-
to-day fans.

A more likely—and potentially positive—role of closed-
circuit television in sports lies in local use, and in the promotion of events that lack the general interest to attract
home-television viewers and sponsors. Pro basketball and
hockey teams have used closed-circuit to handle the overflow
at sellout playoff games; auto races like the Indianapolis 500,
too lengthy for live home-TV coverage, have also prospered
in theaters.

Last week, however, no one in sports seemed able to
think in anything but the grandest terms. The staggering
statistics of the fight promotion competed for headlines with
the event itself. and the over-all effect said as much about
some aspects of the participants as a Woodstock or an Alta-

mont. As if to show that the prevailing greed was shared by almost everyone involved, winner Frazier ended his triumphant night with a brief appearance at a victory party across the street from the Garden. The affair never got off the ground, however, for a simple reason: the man who had just earned $2.5 million by fighting had lent his name to a "party" that welcomed all his admirers—at prices ranging up to $35 a head.

THE MONEYBAGS OF BRITISH SPORT [4]

Sport in Britain today has finally come of age—and it is an age of exploitation. The travelling circus includes professionals, amateurs, shamateurs, agents, impresarios, sponsors, manufacturers, gambling corporations, governing bodies, and government itself. It presents stars, clowns, bright lights and genuine feats of skill and daring. And it all adds up to a lot of money.

Sport has never been a true substitute for war. Indeed in this century we have suffered from a surfeit of both. When Baron de Coubertin reformulated the Olympic ideal in 1908 —"The most important thing in the Olympic Games is not winning but taking part . . . the essential thing in life is not conquering but fighting well"—he could hardly have foreseen that in the 1970s this would be regarded as a pious, fatuous hope with not an inkling of the grim shape of things to come. [It was through the efforts of Pierre, baron de Coubertin, a French educator and sportsman, that the Olympic games were revived, the first meet being held in Athens in 1896. The traditional games of ancient Greece had been discontinued at the end of the first century A.D.—Ed.]. He cannot be blamed for not having had bad dreams, but the strident nationalism and political fanaticism of today's world sports together with the penetration of sport by finance would have bewildered him as much as it did Avery Brundage [until recently, head of the International Olympic Committee]. In

[4] Article by Clifford Makins, former sports editor of the London *Observer*. *New Statesman*. 84:968-70. D. 29, '72. Reprinted by permission.

Britain, gripped by inflation and television, the game is being played for increasingly high stakes.

The man perhaps who controls more of those stakes than anyone else is Mr. Bagenal Harvey. An Irishman from Waterford, he has been the biggest entrepreneur in British sport for more than twenty years. His office—some would say appropriately—lies within sight of Smithfield Meat Market. He looks down from his desk on visitors sitting in low arm-chairs, and if you want to see his monument, look around you. The photographs, cartoons and trophies represent eighty people who qualify as household names. In sports Harvey negotiates television, radio, press and book con-tracts. . . .

In fact Harvey, with a modest staff of ten, has a finger in many succulent pies. His organisation is reckoned to take 10 percent on about £300,000 worth of TV appearances a year. [£1 is worth about $2.40.—Ed.] He is resigned, yet still touchy, about the Mr. X label stuck on him some time ago. It still sticks. Mr. X—why not call him Mr. Harvey?—has been accused of intervening in, or actually setting up, those contractual arrangements between a sportsman who still plays the game and those clubs who employ him to do so. Harvey denies that he has ever meddled in this particular scene. There is one exception. In the case of an overseas player, the celebrated West Indian cricketer, Garfield Sobers, now with Nottinghamshire, Harvey managed the deal. And he agrees that the day is not far off where this rare "ex-ception" might become common practice. He also rebuts the charge of "aggressive marketing" to promote his present clients or to acquire new ones. The initial approach, he says, is always made by the individual or the industry con-cerned. He does not always want the people who want him but he is a shrewd operator with a good ear and a long reach and is not above profitable advice. . . . It may be going too far to suggest that Harvey exercises a stranglehold on this complex, shifting business—just a half nelson perhaps.

Without doubt he is a first-class agent and very few people have joined him and failed to prosper.

Who Sponsors Sports?

On the broad front Harvey says that although industry is ploughing hefty sums into British sport, the net amount that goes to the sport in question, in terms of prize money, better facilities and so on, is relatively small and that the major slice of any given investment is swallowed up in advertising, promotion and entertainment. Maybe. But the motives of sponsors vary. They come in all shapes and sizes with hard and soft centres, with short- and long-term packages, and with vastly differing sums of money.

Consider the field. It includes: *Tobacco*: Wills, Players, Carreras Rothmans, Gallahers (under the banner of Benson and Hedges). *Brewers*: Watneys, Allied Breweries. *Distillers*: Dewars Whisky. *Bookmakers*: William Hill, Ladbrokes, Joe Coral. *Soft Drinks*: Pepsi-Cola and Schweppes. *Petroleum*: Texaco, Esso, BP. *Razor Blades*: Gillette. *Male Cosmetics*: Yardley. *Banks*: Barclays, Midland, Lloyds. *Insurance*: Commercial Union, Norwich Union, Prudential. *Building Societies*: Nationwide. *Trading Stamps*: Green Shield. *Sports Equipment*: Addidas, Puma (based in Germany). *Health Foods*: Bio-Strath. *Diamonds*: de Beers. What comes next is enough to choke a horse or blow a gasket. Between them, these organisations sponsor, promote, support or aid the following sports and recreations: football (soccer), cricket, golf, lawn tennis, table tennis, horse racing, motor racing, pigeon racing, greyhound racing, athletics, show jumping, angling, hockey, snooker, rugby league football, darts, cycling, flying, parachuting, yachting, sailing, canoeing, polo, speedway, rallycross, crown green bowling, and, as an appropriate accompaniment, bagpipes and brass bands. Rugby union, the last outpost of the amateur empire, is still the only major British sport turning down the sponsors. But it is being besieged—or wooed rather, by Watneys. No doubt it will fall in the end.

What does all this cost the sponsors? We shall almost certainly never know the true figure. Some companies are more secretive than others, filling in only part of the expenditure picture; some just don't seem to know. It is a treacherous terrain: shifting sands, in fact, though today's best guess is an annual figure of about £6 million. But some up-to-date figures are available and clearly define the area where the money is going. . . . Watneys spend about £160,000 a year, the majority of this on two football [soccer] competitions in England and Scotland. Pepsi-Cola have just launched a scheme to spend £100,000 on schools football over the next two years in England and Wales. . . . Esso, who gave £25,000 to the British Olympic Appeal Fund are now assisting the Badminton Association to bring over the badminton team of the People's Republic of China. Esso have bought sole advertising rights, and teams will stay at Esso Motor Hotels. It seems plain enough. Whether for good or evil, better or worse, industry is ploughing more and more money into sport. "We are not altruistic," says Mr. Stan Denton of Watneys. "We regard this money as a marketing investment in order to gain certain trade benefits."

Television is the big attraction. The majority of sponsors want to get onto the box where their products in words and slogans, pictures and symbols, flash before a captive audience as the camera pans around and zooms. As one wag neatly put it: "The best thing any government did for sport was to ban cigarette advertising from television." It is a splendid irony. Thrown out of the front door the tobacco companies nipped sharply in again at the back, by way of sport. Even more amazing is that the bulk of this advertising (and it *is* advertising) is now shown on BBC television, which is expressly forbidden by its charter to carry any advertising at all.

Fat Fees for "Columns"

The earnings of British sportsmen in action, apart from the money they get outside the game, is another field of inspired guesswork. There may be fifty footballers earning £200 a week on club contracts alone. Cricketers are not so lucky. . . . Britain's best known boxer, Henry Cooper, admits in a recent autobiography to having earned £50,000 in one good year, apart from those ever-present profitable sidelines. Cooper says: "I enjoyed making commercials and being on television." Britain's richest golfer is Tony Jacklin. He is managed, along with other world-class golfers, by the American Mark McCormack, who expects his clients to earn at least £100,000 a year. Some of these highly paid stars get fat fees for putting their names to newspaper columns and books, often without committing a word to paper. Some of them have serious difficulties with the English language. But their ghost-writers are at hand in the economic machine. Journalists earning between £3,000 and £4,000 a year are instructed and hired by editors and publishers to put words into the mouths of inarticulate, often illiterate men. The formula is neat and cheap: "Star footballer Smith was talking to hack journalist Jones."

Meanwhile transfer fees in football, like the sales of works of art, seem meaningless and insane. . . . The attendances at professional-football matches are down by 270,000 on last season. This simply means that rich clubs will get richer and poor clubs poorer. Fame is the spur. The ultimate dream of many an egocentric millionaire is to run the local club he watched from the terraces as a poor boy.

But there is still a fair appetite for sport in the flesh, a considerable one for sport in the press, and a huge one for sport on television. The press throughout Britain provides a highly specialised coverage in all national, provincial, morning, evening and Sunday newspapers, and the "sports specials." The standards are improving, but with a few notable exceptions are still low. There seems little doubt that the public could easily assimilate higher standards of reporting and interpretation. But . . . the chief sports-reporter does not enjoy the prestige of the chief lobby-correspondent [journalist in the House of Commons], who may write as much tripe as anyone else in the business. "News," like "literature," is regarded as inherently superior. "Sport," which is and should be both, has an inferior status. Television, with the BBC leading the field in expenditure, coverage and expertise, has similar afflictions. Endless teams of experts lead viewers by word and eye. The ceaseless interpretation of trivial incident introduces an element of frenzy and incoherence.

Where government and sport are concerned, policy and principles tend to be well in advance of ready money. But it is an intriguing, important affair that deserves close scrutiny. Those in power and those in opposition may prove to be not too far apart.

Dr. Roger Bannister, who cracked the four-minute mile at Oxford in 1954, with the help of two celebrated Christophers, Chataway and Brasher, is the chairman of the Sports Council, made independent of government by the present administration in the autumn of 1971. As a Fellow of the Royal College of Physicians he has an appropriate air of the senior consultant and looks alarmingly fit. He declares that "Sport has second-class status in the British economy. It is time it moved towards first-class status. At present, if the economy sneezes, sport and recreation catch cold." This echoes the reaction of commercial sponsorship in sport. If the dividends are down, cut the sponsorship.

Millions for Facilities

Last October, after the Sports Council's first year as an independent body, Bannister launched the Sport-for-All Campaign. This was the first step in a ten-year plan "to encourage participation in sport and to improve the facili-

ties for sport." The Council has a target of £350 million
to finance this. "Sport," says Bannister, "is only a part of life,
but it is an essential part of life and should not be treated as
a residual element when it comes to the spending of government or local authority funds."

In Britain at present the total capital investment by local
government outside education in sports facilities for the general public is nearly £20 million a year—compare France
(£63 million) and West Germany (£73 million)—Bannister's Sports Council has a budget of £3.5 million for
England, and another £1 million goes to Scotland and
Wales. This compares with an Arts Council budget of more
than £13.5 million. Bannister certainly needs to exercise
some friendly persuasion on local authorities to attain his
target of £350 million and he must try to screw some more
out of government for his Sports Council budget. One of his
favourite words applied to the role of his Council is catalyst.
Will it, one asks, be able to create chemical and financial
change in other bodies without undergoing change itself?

Mr. Denis Howell, Opposition spokesman on sport, has
his doubts. When Labour was in power Howell was both
the Minister for Sport and the chairman of the Sports Council. A top Football League referee in his day who knew
several ways of telling a player that he was guilty of un-
gentlemanly conduct, Howell points out that the Royal
Charter granted to Bannister's independent Sports Council
is simply a device to give money to a body that need not
come to Parliament for legislation. . . . The government, he
says, is more or less standing still on the policies and finance
initiated in his time. The £3 million he had for the Sports
Council is now £4.5 million. Given the inflation factor
there is little advance. He approves Bannister's policy of
trying to create multisports centres but thinks this may be
unfair to individual sports.

Government's Role

Mr. Eldon Griffiths, member for Bury St. Edmunds, Joint Parliamentary Under-Secretary of State of the Environment and Minister for Sport, has a high-rise suite of offices in Westminster. Like Dr. Bannister he has a slight tendency to tell you what he thinks rather than answer what you want to know. But he is sharp, definite and well briefed.

He thinks that Bannister's Sports Council is now exactly where it ought to have been in the first place—outside government and left to get on with its own job: "to be free to bring its own pressure on government." The ministerial accountability is there of course, but not on a day-to-day management basis. Griffiths was both optimistic and cautious about Bannister's target of £350 million. If there are no unforeseen setbacks in the economy there should be no problem. He pressed on with his philosophy of sport and recreation. Although "government has a role in the encouragement of excellence" the production of Olympic champions should play a secondary role to the provision of better facilities for sport and recreation for all members of the community. The Sports Council does not exist "to promote the hard sports; it should be concerned with leisure and recreation for people of all ages; they should be free to do their own thing."

He stressed that the government is encouraging the better use of educational plant in schools and colleges and is using the space and facilities of the armed services; and in the sector of public industry it seeks wider access to reservoirs, Forestry Commission lands and the countryside. In the sector of private industry it seeks the use of the facilities of huge companies. . . .

As for the money put into sport to promote smoking and drinking, Mr. Griffiths argues that too much stress can be put on this as a moral issue. One sympathises. Most people do not smoke and drink—any more than they shave themselves—to death. Meanwhile the Exchequer receives an annual revenue of £1,142 million on tobacco, £999 million on drink, and a tax income of £150 million on all gaming, betting and pools.

Sport and money are irrevocably locked together in Britain today. Those who play the game want to be paid more and more for it. There are few footballers and cricketers in the land who would not rejoice to hear that the rewards of winning Cup Finals and Test Matches were to be increased tenfold because these sacred occasions had fallen into the hands of a free-spending captain of industry. Definition must precede blame, but there is always something disturbing about those, whether individuals or corporations, who exploit rather than explore.

IV. THE PLAYERS

EDITOR'S INTRODUCTION

As fans, of course, our sympathies go out to the players. Standing often alone—against the magnates who own them, occasionally quitting the game rather than sell themselves short, struggling endlessly for the right to control their own careers and win their just rewards—what could be more appealing than the manipulated athlete taking his dramatic stand against the forces of money and power that are said to control him? And yet, somehow, the picture doesn't quite fit. That athlete is often as tycoon-minded as his boss. He is sometimes as greedy as the greed merchants who are said to dominate him. And how is it, anyway, that a man who is privileged to live out the dreams, the not-so-secret fantasies, of boyhood would sooner quit the game than work for $150,000? There is something outrageous in such behavior, though we are occasionally hard pressed to put our fingers on what it is. Perhaps athletes should be judged as commodities, after all. The majority of them appear to believe they are worth solely what the market will bear—if the market weren't rigged.

This section is designed as a counterbalance to the views of those who believe that the ruination of sports lies at the door of the accountants and money managers, wholly and solely. As the first contribution, by Pete Axthelm, sports editor of *Newsweek*, makes clear, the athletes themselves are shrewdly doing their bit. Here we meet not the anonymous money managers of the teams and owners but the well-publicized managers of the prime athletes themselves, whose incorporated assets occasionally outdo those of a modest industrial enterprise. The lesson, says Axthelm, is brief and to the point: "It matters not whether you win or lose, but how you've chosen your business manager."

The next article, from *Ebony,* provides a rundown of player salaries and bargaining principles in a typical year. The numbers of athletes reported as running well over the $100,000-a-year mark indicate how well the bargaining is going. In the third article a basketball superstar recounts his own financial maneuverings toward a place in the sun and asserts that there have to be some standards and ceilings established for money paid to athletes. "The players," he notes sympathetically, "naturally, have been trying to get all they can and the owners, carried away by the competition, are in danger of being carried away in boxes."

In the final article, *Time* magazine recounts the exploits of a "Jeremiah of Jock Liberation" who has dedicated himself to freeing (and organizing) athletes against the power of the money crowd. His essential message—"You can be a human being without sacrificing quality"—is something of a shocker in itself.

ATHLETES OR TYCOONS? [1]

During O. J. Simpson's rookie year in professional football as a running back for the Buffalo Bills, he also made his début as a rookie actor on a television show called *Medical Center.* The reviews were good—better, cynics might have pointed out, than some of the reviews of his performances on the field—and several producers sent him inquiries and scripts. One project intrigued him; he was offered the part of a Black militant in a heated drama that ended with a ghetto street in flames. O. J. showed the script to his business manager, Chuck Barnes.

"Sure it's good," said Barnes. "And as long as you play the part, you might as well go out in the street and throw Royal Crown Cola bottles through the windows of Chevrolet showrooms."

[1] From "Men Behind the Men Who Make Money in Sports," by Pete Axthelm, sports editor for *Newsweek. Vogue.* 157:186-7+. My. '71. Copyright © 1971 by Pete Axthelm. Reprinted by permission of The Sterling Lord Agency, Inc.

If the answer was somewhat facetious—neither Simpson nor Barnes really believed that anyone would take a mere acting rôle that seriously—it was also indicative of the thought processes of the men behind today's wealthiest athletes. Barnes feels he must weigh every business decision against O. J.'s lucrative contracts with firms like Royal Crown and Chevrolet. After all, he is being paid to market a product named O. J. Simpson, and he insists on controlling the exposure and distribution of that product. Barnes calls his approach "total management"; in two years it has made O. J. a millionaire.

Barnes, whose Sports Headliners Inc. has offices in Indianapolis and Los Angeles, is one of the best-known figures in a rapidly expanding sports profession. As sports have become increasingly big businesses, business managers have inevitably grown more important. Many such men are the fast-talking flesh-peddlers who have always lurked on the fringes of sport, hoping to snare 10 percent of some young athlete's bonus money and get out of sight. But at the other extreme, such people as Barnes and Mark McCormack direct vast and meticulously planned financial empires for their clients. They are not agents, they emphasize, but managers. And their concepts have altered the economics of the entire sporting scene.

McCormack, a Cleveland lawyer and confessed golf nut, started the modern area of sports management when he began representing Arnold Palmer in 1959. As a participant sport played by affluent consumers, golf probably provided the ideal testing ground for a would-be sports merchandiser; but no one could have anticipated McCormack's stunning success. Before joining McCormack, Palmer enjoyed a few traditional endorsement contracts and a total annual income of around $60,000. McCormack junked the endorsements and set up whole new companies in Palmer's name. Within a few years the true Palmer fan could swing Arnie's clubs, wear his sportswear and get it cleaned at his laundries.

Palmer's income was estimated at more than half a million dollars, but even that was beneath McCormack's concerns; he spoke instead of long-range benefits at lower taxes and of equity and net worth—which was clearly in the millions.

The Palmer boom didn't go unnoticed among his fellow pros, and soon Jack Nicklaus and Gary Player had also joined McCormack, giving him total control of golf's "Big Three." A dozen or so lesser stars back up McCormack's front line, and he has recently ventured into such sports as skiing (Jean-Claude Killy) and pro football ([former] New York Giant Fran Tarkenton).

Barnes launched his own empire in 1964, in another sport that offered great riches in products and endorsements —auto racing. Before Barnes's arrival, many drivers had been content to slap various oil, gas, tire, and parts decals on their cars for modest fees and free equipment; Barnes convinced such champions as Parnelli Jones, Mario Andretti, and A. J. Foyt that they were worth far more. Soon the drivers were looking into pizza franchises and auto service centers as well as lucrative contracts with auto manufacturers —and Barnes was seeking new challenges in pro football.

Some Advice Can Be Bad

The football fields were already littered with the casualties of the war between the National and American leagues. Among other effects, that fierce bidding battle for talent had attracted legions of new agents and lawyers. A few had helped young stars to play the leagues against one another to grab huge bonuses; others merely took advantage of circumstances and accepted credit for contracts that would have been paid in any case at the height of the war. Joe Namath's case illustrates the latter phenomenon. Namath placed undying faith in the men who won his $400,000 contract with the New York Jets, forgetting that Jets' president Sonny Werblin *wanted* to pay a record price for the publicity value. And as he struggled through a disastrous fast-food franchise

operation as well as his near-retirement over his Bachelors
III bar, Namath continued to listen to his young yes-men.
At one point Werblin, the former president of the Music
Corporation of America and one of the most successful agents
of all time, tried to aid Namath, only to have one of Joe's
young lawyers question Werblin's business judgment.

Entering after the merger between the leagues had ended
the inflated bidding for players, Barnes could afford no
mistakes with his most publicized client, Simpson. As O. J.'s
negotiations with Buffalo stalled, Barnes called on every
power of persuasion or threat; but ultimately he knew he
would have to take less than he wanted, because so many
outside deals depended on O. J.'s playing ball. The contract
Simpson signed was hardly a capitulation—he's getting at
least $250,000 for four years and a $100,000 loan—but it provided only a minor percentage of O. J.'s income. As Mc-
Cormack had done with his golfers, Barnes had transformed
Simpson into a one-man financial boom.

If the trend toward management was born in such individual sports as golf and auto racing, then fueled by the
league wars in football and later basketball, it is finally making inroads into the more entrenched and monopolistic
sports. A Toronto lawyer named Alan Eagleson has almost
singlehandedly dismantled ice hockey's feudal structure.
[See "Hockey Hits the Big Time," in Section I, above.] Once,
young skaters were swept into big-league organizations as
teen-agers and expected to be grateful for any salaries the
parent club might eventually grant. Representing individuals as well as The Players' Association, Eagleson has given
the players a new voice and sent salaries spiralling.

Eagleson and his flamboyant counterparts in other sports
arouse rage among club owners and other traditionalists; but
having experienced the joys of increased power and higher
salaries, the players are never going to be without the Eagle-
sons again. Nor will they turn away from such money managers as McCormack and Barnes, who can parlay relatively

short athletic careers into comfortable lifetimes. Palmer went
fourteen months without winning a tournament; Simpson
suffered two sub-par seasons—and both continued to ring up
six-figure profits. Others have played better and earned far
less, but that only bears out a fact of sporting life in the
1970s: It matters not whether you win or lose, but how
you've chosen your business manager.

HOW MUCH IS A PLAYER WORTH? [2]

How much is a major-league baseball player worth? As
a man, he's priceless. But as a baseball player, by tradition,
he's worth as little as the general manager, with the bene-
diction of the reserve clause, will convince him to sign for.

Each year, between October and April, six hundred major-league baseball players make their pilgrimages to front
offices to talk contract. Mr. Average Player comes alone, carrying a wrinkled piece of paper on which are the raw di-
mensions of next year's salary.

"How much are you worth?" the general manager asks.

"I'm a four-year veteran," says Mr. Average Player. "I
have a career batting average of .250, 65 RBIs, 14 homers and
145 hits. I signed autographs last year. I was real good to
the press and I never gave the front office any trouble. I
think I deserve $30,000."

"That's much more than I had in mind," says the general
manager. "I figured $20,000."

"But look what I've done for the club already," pleads
Mr. Average Player.

"Yeh," says the general manager. "But what are you
going to do for me next year? Suppose you break a leg."

Mr. Average Player scratches his head. He disagrees with
the general manager, but he can think of nothing more to
say. After all, generally young and poor, he is called the
"unsophisticate" of the pro sports world. His "college pro-

[2] Article in *Ebony*. 27:152-4+. Je. '72. Reprinted by permission of *Ebony*
Magazine, copyright 1972 by Johnson Publishing Company, Inc.

fessors," after he finished high school, were the old coaches of minor-league baseball back in Tidewater, Waterbury and Danville and they unfortunately had taught him how to play ball "for" but never "with" the front office.

A few more words are exchanged before Mr. Average Player walks out with a $23,500 contract in hand.

For some 95 percent of major-league baseball players, this is usually the gist of contract negotiations. The exceptions are the gutsy holdouts and the select superstars who send an agent or lawyers to negotiate contracts for them while they sit back, sip beer and watch TV at home.

A major exception was Oakland Athletics pitcher Vida Blue. Last year [1971], when the rookie sensation wasn't seen live working on his phenomenal 24-8 record, he was starring in TV commercials, such as one for a popular after-shave lotion in which he said, with a smile and soft, smooth voice, "you've probably heard [from no less an authority than President Richard Nixon] that I'm the most underpaid superstar in baseball. But next year, I'm going to be making a whoooleeeoootamoney."

The Revolt of Vida Blue

In his first full year with the Athletics, Blue received a salary of $14,750, plus such tokens as a $10,000 Cadillac and use of a couple of A's owner Charles Finley's credit cards for some $3,500 worth of sundry items. Finley offered Blue $50,000 this year. But Blue was heavily credited, by his lawyer Robert Gerst and by Finley, for having increased A's home attendance by 136,000, club road-attendance by 250,000, its revenue by $500,000 and the worth of the A's franchise by $2 million. Thus, the discrepancy between his obvious worth (a reported $1.2 million league-asset) and his official wage prompted Blue and Gerst to initially demand $115,000 before trimming it to $75,000 and they had hoped the coin of contractual fate would flip in their favor.

On one side of the coin was the traditional minimum salary (which is $13,500 today) and giving him an average annual raise of 20 percent, depending on the player's progress as an athlete, a front-office cheerleader and a gate influence, and also depending upon his ability to bargain. At this rate, it would have taken Blue five straight similar seasons to reach the 100 Grand Club.

On the other side of the coin was the proposed revolutionary method of paying a baseball player a reasonable salary for what he is worth *today*. This policy, in Blue's case, would acknowledge last year's salary as a residual and his new contract as a true salary reflecting his proven worth. If Blue is worth $500,000 to Finley, and Finley says he is, then why can't Blue get the $75,000 contract he finally asked for? The $425,000 balance for Finley is an awfully good deal and the other league owners can continue sharing the $700,000 Blue is said to have generated for them through sell-out crowds on the road.

"What we're trying to do is get rid of the fallacy that a salary should be based on number of years in the game," says Gerst. "Blue is already one of baseball's top-ten pitchers. He should be paid accordingly."

Blue had but two choices: accept Finley's offer or retire from baseball. Blue chose to retire and to sign on as a public relations man with Dura Steel Products Company, for a salary exceeding $50,000. The company immediately got about $1 million worth of free publicity by riding Blue's headlines.

Baseball players, in general, feel that the pay system is fair, that the best players make the most money and that a player's progress is usually reflected in his paycheck. In an informal poll by *Ebony*, most players said they even felt Finley's offer was an extraordinary salary for a second-year man, that Blue could make $100,000 on the side in endorsements and that he would be better able to collect $75,000 or even $90,000 if he would have another equally good year.

Ralph Garr, nicknamed Roadrunner because of his blaz-
ing speed, earned about $13,500 . . . in his first full season
as an Atlanta Braves outfielder. By season's end, he had
sprayed 219 hits on enemy pitchers, had stolen 30 bases and
had scored 101 runs enroute to a .343 batting average, second
highest in major-league baseball. He got a raise to $40,000
this year.

Earl Williams, a teammate of Garr, won the National
League's Rookie of the Year honor . . . [in 1971], scoring 64
runs, hitting 33 homers and driving in 87 runs. His home-run
and RBI totals were each the second highest ever for National League rookies. For this, Williams' salary jumped
from $12,750 to $37,000, a raise of almost 300 percent.

Chicago Cubs pitcher Ferguson Jenkins won 24 games
and lost 13 . . . [in 1971], the fifth straight year he'd won
twenty or more. He copped the Cy Young Award, among several other honors, and his was the club's most sparkling
performance though the Cubs failed to win a pennant. For
such achievements, Jenkins was given a salary raise from
$90,000 to $125,000 a year for the next two seasons.

After a lengthy holdout, Dick Allen signed a $135,000
contract with the Chicago White Sox. The salary is a $30,000
increase over last year's but it is considered compensation
for his big bat, for his crowd-drawing power and for the
agony and inconvenience of being traded the third straight
year. Allen's courage, as well as his physical talent and intelligence, enable him to say more about his professional
worth than most players.

$200,000 a Year

Perhaps the man who has the most control over his professional worth as a baseball player is Hank (The Hammer)
Aaron, the game's greatest power slugger alive. The Atlanta
Braves outfielder has more than 3,000 hits, more than 630
homers and a .313 batting average over eighteen years. He
has every chance of breaking Babe Ruth's coveted career
home-run record of 714. For his talent and destined crowd-

drawing appeal, he has been awarded a $200,000 salary, highest in baseball history, for each of the next three years.

Not only does everyone in baseball agree that Hank, more than anyone else, is worth that salary, many feel he is worth more. "Aaron is worth $400,000," says Billy Conigliaro.

"He deserves every bit of it," says Baltimore's Paul Blair, "not just for what he's going to do but for what he has been doing for years without being adequately paid."

A man is entitled to ask for what he feels he's worth [says Aaron]. But one never feels he's completely paid what he's worth. In general, I feel baseball's pay is fair. Baseball is seldom an overnight success, and the pay system is structured to make a man prove himself before he enters the big-dollar bracket. Management knows that, once a player reaches a huge salary, it can't be cut more than 20 percent over one year or more than 30 percent over two.

Consistency is the key to a baseball player's financial worth [Aaron continues]. The owner also looks at what a player contributes to the sport off the field. As for the Vida Blue case, I think he deserves as much as he can get. A lot of people don't realize the average baseball-career lasts only four years, and that a man is real lucky if he plays ten or more years. Vida Blue had a good year in '71, but next year his arm could go sour and keep him from capitalizing on the season he has already had. Still again, you got to also look at it from the owner's side. I believe I'm worth every bit of my contract, but I also realize that management has taken a risk. What if I get injured and have to retire next year?

To be sure, Blue and Aaron represent both extremes of a baseball player's bargaining situation. Blue is an overnight sensation. Aaron is a veteran superstar, who came up through the ranks and only recently (three years ago) began to make the top dollar. But for every Vida Blue and Hank Aaron there are a dozen other players earning much less.

Because of relatively high player salaries and huge owner profits, many fans believe that both the owners and the players are "overpaid" for the amount of work they do, and that the recent player strike and other financial controversies reveal a mutual greediness. Owners say they can't afford to pay much because baseball is a marginal enterprise. Yet the

Cleveland Indians, one of baseball's weakest franchises, is being sold for $10 million. The average franchise reportedly reaps roughly $1.5 million in annual pre-tax profits, of which $700,000 pay salaries for twenty-five players, averaging $28,500 a man.

There are twenty-three players making $100,000 a year in baseball today [mid-1972]. Although St. Louis and San Francisco have three each, there are ten clubs with none. The 100-grand players are: Hank Aaron of the Atlanta Braves, $200,000; Carl Yastrzemski, $165,000 and Luis Aparicio, $100,000, Boston Red Sox; Fergie Jenkins, $125,000 and Billy Williams, $115,000, Chicago Cubs; Roberto Clemente, $150,000, Pittsburgh Pirates [Clemente died in a plane crash December 31, 1972.—Ed.]; Dick Allen, $135,000, Chicago White Sox; Juan Marichal, $140,000, Willie Mays, $165,000 and Willie McCovey, $120,000, San Francisco Giants; Frank Robinson, $140,000 and Maury Wills, $100,000, Los Angeles Dodgers; Tom Seaver, $120,000, New York Mets; Harmon Killebrew, $125,000 and Tony Oliva, $105,000, Minnesota Twins; Frank Howard, $120,000, Texas Rangers; Bob Gibson, $150,000, Joe Torre, $140,000 and Lou Brock, $110,000, St. Louis Cardinals; Pete Rose, $110,000, Cincinnati Reds; Al Kaline, $110,000, Detroit Tigers; Brooks Robinson, $110,000 and Dave McNally, $105,000, Baltimore Orioles.

Although most of the six hundred players (including 165 blacks) contend the pay is fair, the system for deriving the figures is surely one-sided. The player is limited in his bargaining power and the only financial indication of his professional worth is what the owner has agreed to pay. Because of the reserve clause, the professional lives of twenty-five men are the monopoly of one man—the owner. Until the Supreme Court or some appropriate force changes the system, the Vida Blue case proves that there will always be doubt about the real worth of a major-league baseball player, from the standpoint of money, and also from the standpoint of manhood.

CONFESSIONS OF A BASKETBALL STAR [3]

If I have become a gypsy, it is because I lie down with gypsies. Jumping to a franchise in Oakland, I landed in a franchise that landed in Washington and then in Virginia and now operates out of Norfolk, Richmond, Roanoke and Hampton. I did not have to go with the team to Virginia or I would have had a lot more home cities to add to my collection. As it is, since I left Roselle Park [New Jersey] High School, I have played with the Miami University Hurricanes, San Francisco Warriors, Oakland Oaks, Washington Caps and New York Nets. I have worn a wide variety of uniforms, but at least I was never traded or sold without my insistence.

I am supposed to be wrong for jumping from team to team, yet it is supposed to be all right for teams to trade or sell players from team to team. Also, it is not supposed to be right for a player to jump from one town to another, but it is all right for an owner to do so. It is all right for a franchise to be taken away from Oakland and put in Washington and taken away from Washington and put in Virginia. It is all right for the St. Louis owner to put his team and coach and players out of St. Louis and into Atlanta. It is all right for an owner to take a team out of San Diego and put it in Houston. Or take a team out of San Francisco and put it in Oakland. It is all right for major-league baseball to take a team out of Milwaukee and put it in Atlanta and put a team in Seattle and then take it out and put it in Milwaukee.

Is There a Double Standard?

I could go on, but you must get the message. We operate on a double standard. What is all right for leagues is not all right for individuals, what is all right for employers is not all right for employees. I'm sorry, but I don't agree. And I really don't think you would if you were in my place. I am

[3] From the book Confessions of a Basketball Gypsy: The Rick Barry Story, by Rick Barry with Bill Libby. Prentice-Hall. '72. p 273-86. © 1972 by Rick Barry and Bill Libby. Published by Prentice-Hall, Inc., Englewood Cliffs, N.J. Rick Barry has been a star with both the National Basketball Association and the American Basketball Association.

not saying some of the things I did might not have been wrong, or that two wrongs make a right. I simply am saying I am a prisoner of the system, so I have used the system and tried to beat the big boys at their own game. I have not entirely succeeded, but that is my tough luck. In the end, I have not done too bad.

Some move around in sports by choice. And some are kicked around. Sometimes it's a little of both. My old coach, Alex Hannum, played in Oshkosh, Anderson, Syracuse, Baltimore, Rochester, Milwaukee, Fort Wayne and St. Louis, and has coached in St. Louis, Rochester, Syracuse, Philadelphia, San Francisco, Oakland, San Diego and now Denver. Can he condemn me? We are kings of the road, transients who tour and ply our trade from town to town. It is what I wanted to avoid, but jumped into. It's nothing but a floating crap game, and for a longtime I was losing. . . .

When I jumped, not many followed me. But then Zemo Beaty jumped to Utah and Joe Caldwell jumped from Atlanta to Carolina. Even though it appears Dave Bing and Bill Cunningham will not make the jumps they contracted to make, there had been enough prominent players jumping to make the NBA [National Basketball Association] jump. Then Spencer Haywood jumped from the ABA [American Basketball Association] to the NBA and the ABA got jumpy. Obviously I am not the only player out to better myself.

Pro Basketball Enters a Boom

This jumping was a big thing that made a merger attractive to the two leagues. Another big thing came when the ABA finally began to sign college stars such as Dan Issel and Charley Scott for last season and Artis Gilmore and Jim McDaniels for this season. With the continued development of such established ABA players as Mel Daniels and John Brisker, it is clear the ABA has a depth of talent now far superior to what it had when I entered the league.

The better teams, such as Utah, Kentucky and Indiana, will prove competitive with many NBA teams first chance they get. And if they are not as good as the best, they have the base on which to build up to the best. The key thing is that some of the best big men have come into the ABA now, fellows who eventually may enable some of our teams to beat out the teams with Lew Alcindor [now called Kareem Abdul-Jabbar], Willis Reed, Wilt Chamberlain and Nate Thurmond.

One of the main problems with the expansion of pro basketball is that there seldom have been more than five or six outstanding big centers at any one time, and without a big center you cannot win much.

If the merger comes off as the leagues are presently constituted, there would be twenty-eight franchises in more than thirty cities. One city, New York, would have two teams. A number of cities in a number of states, such as North Carolina and Virginia, would share their teams. Not all are equal to it, though there may still be some cities not in pro basketball that could support teams. As it is, few are turning a profit. However, a few more seem to be moving into the black every season. New York and Los Angeles have been big pro basketball towns for years, and lately Milwaukee, Chicago, Detroit and Phoenix have picked up. In the ABA, Indianapolis and Louisville have been solid, and now Salt Lake City has come on strong.

It is a great game and seems to be close to a boom period such as pro football entered a few years back, so perhaps pessimism is out of line. It is not illogical to envision pro basketball as the next big sport in this country.

I presume the merger would help this, although most players are against it. I am for it, but I understand their reasoning. A merger might weigh against free enterprise, for which I have fought and been branded a bum. When the merger comes, I hope it comes with a new set of rules that free the players from slavery.

Slavery Is Slavery

And slavery is slavery, no matter what the slave is paid. It's fantastic to be making $100,000 or more, but it also would be nice to be able to seek more elsewhere or choose the firm you want to work for or the town you want to live in. Salesmen can. And plumbers. And broadcasters. And sportswriters. No one screamed bloody murder when a number of outstanding referees jumped from the NBA to the ABA, but aren't they as important as players? They went where they felt it would be better for them. More power to them. Many big businessmen make more money than top athletes and yet have far greater freedom of movement and choice. Fair is fair, whatever the fee.

It was unfair and, as the courts have ruled, illegal for pro leagues to rule that a fellow could not play pro ball until his college class graduated. The ABA claimed it was all right for Denver to sign Spencer Haywood and Ralph Simpson because they had personal "hardship cases," but they should not have had to make any excuses, and a fringe result of Haywood's court fight freeing him to jump from the ABA to the NBA was that there need not be any such excuses anymore.

Personally, I think everyone should want to go to college and to study and to graduate from college with training for a profession, but the fact is many athletes have had no interest in college, were there, branded as "college bums," only because it was the only road to the pros, and while there, were denied a lot of money they might have made as pros. Now, a George McGinnis is free to leave Indiana University and join the Indiana Pacers if he wishes, as he did. Just as a law student is free to quit and become a professional singer if he wants.

If there is a merger, I hope it comes without a common draft and with a rule giving veterans some freedom. I can understand that the leagues feel they could not operate on a stable basis if players are forever free to jump from team to team. However, if athletes cannot choose the organization they want to join and the city they want to live in, as can persons in other professions, if there is no common draft they at least will have two teams and cities from which to choose. And if a player gets in some seniority—say, three to five years—and is then free to make a move to a team that will pay him more or to a town he prefers, he is not stuck for his entire career in a spot he may dislike. I don't see why the reserve clause can't be modified in this way.

It simply isn't fair when a player lands in a small city or with a team that isn't drawing and the owner says he can't afford to pay him what New York or L.A. can, yet the player has no chance to offer his services to New York or L.A. The San Francisco columnist who criticizes those like me who seek greener pastures has probably spent his journalism career taking more attractive offers in other towns as they came up.

Need for a Ceiling on Pro Wages

However—and this may shock you—it also seems to me there have to be some standards and ceilings established for money paid to athletes. The players, naturally, have been trying to get all they can and the owners, carried away by the competition, are in danger of being carried away in boxes. Bonuses and salaries have been spiraling beyond reasonable levels, and once this has begun it's awfully hard to stop. It's easy to say owners wouldn't pay what they couldn't afford, but what I'm afraid of is franchises will fold and jobs will be lost. I think a merger is essential to the health of pro basketball. It is that simple.

Although fewer teams in pro basketball are making a profit than teams in most other pro sports, pro basketball players are now the highest-paid athletes. College players get million-dollar contracts before they even prove they can play pro ball, although many of these contracts are so complicated it is far from clear whether they will wind up with what they believe they'll get. There are guys in big-league basketball collecting $50,000 a season who aren't good enough to make the road trips. And there are more $100,000 performers than in any other sport.

It requires some guessing on my part, but I believe that players who are making $100,000 or more a season or are about to move into this class include Wilt Chamberlain, Jerry West, Elgin Baylor, Nate Thurmond, Oscar Robertson, Lew Alcindor, Elvin Hayes, Connie Hawkins, Willis Reed, Walt Frazier, Bill Bradley, Cazzie Russell, Dave Bing, Billy Cunningham, Wes Unseld, Spencer Haywood, Zelmo Beaty, Mel Daniels and Roger Brown, to say nothing of players such as Pete Maravich, Bob Lanier, Charley Scott, Rick Mount, Dan Issel, Curtis Rowe, Artis Gilmore, Jim Mc-Daniels and others who signed long-term bonus contracts out of college the last couple of years. I belong in this class, too, though I just entered the $100,000 category last season. And some have entered or may soon enter the $200,000 class.

It is possible a limit should be set on the bonus and salary permitted a new player until he has proven himself, so it is the choice of teams and cities, not the amount of money he can get on the auction block, which is granted him in the freedom of a dual draft. Players should have to earn the money they make, and possibly there should be reasonable ceilings established based on seniority as well as performance, which would be the same regardless of the city in which the player lands. Many players would oppose this, I'm sure. I want to make what players of comparable seniority and performance are getting, but I do not want to break any franchises. . . .

Fame—and Bitterness

Being in sports has altered me a great deal. It has brought me fame, honors and luxury. It has also turned me hard and made me a bit bitter. Only now in New York is the bitterness easing and am I beginning to relax. In some ways my personality has changed for the better. I'm more outgoing. I try harder not to alienate people and to reach out to those who only want to be kind to me. I'm more respectful of my family. I always loved my wife and kids, but now I know better how much they mean to me and how much they've given up for me. I'm still a difficult character, temperamental and hard to live with and somewhat selfish, but I'm better than I was.

I'm better organized. I hired managers to invest my money and get me deals for side money. They have set up and are setting up only solid investments, not get-rich-quick schemes. While I was attached to the West Coast, these advisers were Al Ross of All-Pro Management in Century City, a very sharp attorney, and his brother Leonard and Barry Marlin of Marlin and Ross of L.A. Now that I'm on the East Coast, my business is being conducted by Marty Litke of the Will Morris Agency. It looks like I will be doing more and more television work in the future, which I love. And there are other business matters brewing that appear promising.

THE PLAYERS FIGHT BACK [4]

"It did not take a genius," says Jack Scott, director of the Institute for the Study of Sport and Society, "to see a couple of years ago that the counterculture was going to have an impact on the nation's athletics, one of the most conservative, narrow and encrusted segments of our society." It did take a kind of Jock Jeremiah, though, to spread the word and to preach the gospel of locker-room dissent. That Scott has done. After teaching a course called Intercollegiate Athletics and Education: A Socio-Psychological Evaluation at the University of California at Berkeley . . . he founded his nonprofit institute to hold seminars, publish a newsletter and "help interpret what's going on in sport and make it what it can and should be." His new book, called *The Athletic Revolution,* is long on rhetoric and short on solutions, but its compilation of articles, speeches

[4] From "Jeremiah of Jock Liberation." *Time*. 87:88-9+. My. 24, '71. Reprinted by permission from *Time*, The Weekly Newsmagazine; Copyright Time Inc.

and case histories is nonetheless the most penetrating of the spate of recent books that question not only the structure but the philosophy of sports.

Scott, twenty-nine, a 9.6 man in the 100-yard dash before an arthritic ankle cut short his track career at Stanford, contends that the "quasi-militaristic manner" in which "racist, insensitive" coaches coerce their "captive athletes" robs sport of its "best justification—that it is fun to do." The problem, he says, is that "sport in America is more spectator- than participant-oriented." Though he allows that competition is necessary to develop talent, he emphasizes that

the process of sport is more important than the product. The beauty is in the classic struggle of man against man, man against nature and man against himself. The index of how well you do is how well you struggle. If you don't struggle well, you should feel badly. But you shouldn't feel badly just because you lose. The final score should be almost incidental.

Scott's thesis would be scorned by such hard-nosed coaches as Leo Durocher ("Nice guys finish last") or the late Vince Lombardi ("Winning isn't everything; it's the *only* thing"). Though Scott is primarily interested in reforming college athletics, the ramification of his ideas nevertheless carries through all sports, from the professional game right down to the Little League. When Dave Meggyesy quit his $35,000 job as linebacker for the St. Louis Cardinals . . . he holed up in Scott's apartment for four months to write *Out of Their League*. The book is an angry, sometimes self-righteous attack on the "incredible racism," "dehumanizing conditions" and "violence and sadism" of pro football. Sparing no one, Meggyesy rails against coaches, trainers, who "do more dealing in drugs than the average junkie," and players, one of whom (Jim Ringo, former All-League center for Lombardi's Green Bay Packers) supposedly told Meggyesy in all seriousness that "in football the Commies are on one side of the ball and we're on the other."

Prolonged Adolescence

The sport establishment—coaches, athletic directors, team owners, league officials—usually tries to dismiss its critics as a few isolated malcontents; but the charge simply doesn't wash. In *The Athletic Revolution,* Scott notes that since 1967 the athletics programs at more than one hundred schools "have been rocked by some form of disturbance." Most have involved athletes, protesting what they consider racism and unfair disciplinary rules. The extent of what Scott calls "the turmoil in sport" does not stop with amateurs. . . . [In April 1971] no less a pro star than George Sauer, the brilliant wide-receiver for the New York Jets, announced that he was quitting football because it "works to mold you into someone easy to manipulate." With Scott coaching from the sidelines, Sauer said he loved the game but not the "system" that tries "to keep players in a prolonged state of adolescence."

It could be argued, of course, that instead of dropping out, a reform-minded athlete would be more effective working from within, through the increasingly militant players' associations. Though Sauer made his announcement through the Institute for the Study of Sport and Society, Scott says that he did not urge Sauer to quit but simply "helped him make the transition from jock back to human being." Scott's critics scoff at his institute as a kind of halfway house for troubled athletes (in fact, it is a family operation which Scott and his wife Micki run out of an office above his apartment in Oakland, California). They regard his work as inconsequential if not unfair—and indeed Scott is sometimes given to excess. In an earlier book called *Athletics for Athletes,* he delivered the sweeping and undocumented charge that too many coaches "have problems with latent homosexuality."

Nonetheless, the movement that Scott represents cannot be easily dismissed. The aspects of sport he explores in his book—racism, "shamateurism," drug abuse, dictatorial coaches, overemphasis on winning, the role of athletics in education—are problems that organized sports, like it or not, must grapple with in the 1970s.

It will be a long, hard struggle. Marshaled against jock liberation is what Scott calls the "paternalistic authoritarianism" of the sport establishment. "The dominant philosophy in American athletics," as Scott calls it, is summed up in a speech by Max Rafferty, the former California State Superintendent of Public Instruction. At a conference of athletic directors, Rafferty, a onetime high school football coach, allowed that "there are two great national institutions which simply cannot tolerate either internal dissension or external interference: our armed forces and our interscholastic sports program. Both are of necessity benevolent dictatorships." Describing athletes as "decent, reasonably patriotic Americans" who are "under increasing attack from the kooks, crumbums and Commies," he avowed his love of sports as symbolizing "the clean, bright, fighting spirit which is America itself." Rafferty, reports Scott, was given a standing ovation.

Joyous Activity

Organized sport will undoubtedly continue to move away from Rafferty's ideal of a benevolent dictatorship; but it will surely fall somewhere short of Scott's grandiose vision of "a humane, just society in which sport will flourish as a meaningful, joyous activity." In the era of Joe Namath, the old image of the sports hero as a crew-cut, Wheaties-eating, All-American boy is fast fading, as are many of the petty restrictions on an athlete's life-style. What will linger is the traditional ethic that winning is synonymous with success. At colleges where alumni contributions have a way of varying in direct relationship to the success of the football team, coaches who value their jobs will still strive to win at almost any cost. Among the pros, where players are supposedly beyond the age of character building, sport will remain spectator-oriented for as long as admission is charged.

If winning is to be an end in itself, Scott would like to change the means to that end. "Lombardi and the other over-authoritarian coaches have proved that heavy discipline can produce winners," he says. "But it is also possible to learn and develop in a more free and creative atmosphere. You can be a human being without sacrificing quality." Such is the struggle that sports will play out in the 1970s. The opening whistle in fact has just sounded.

V. ALL THAT GLITTERS . . .

EDITOR'S INTRODUCTION

Maybe money matters hold such a supreme place in sports because financial problems are so critical. It is a thought worth considering. A number of the articles in preceding sections have emphasized the all-consuming drive for a sound financial reward as a chief motivation of the sports industry today. This section is designed to impart the message that what glitters is not necessarily gold. For all the muckraking, for all the talk of the Money God, there are a number of teams in every league that would close down tomorrow were profit the sole motive of the enterprise.

As an excerpt from *U.S. News & World Report* points out, the days of big profits in pro sports appear to be ending, and about half of all pro teams are losing money. Hockey, horse racing, golf, pro football, and even car racing seem to be doing well, but baseball and basketball are in considerable trouble—and the trouble could shift to other sports in the years ahead. The financially astute *Wall Street Journal,* seconding the view, quotes two brothers, Gerald and Allan Phipps, who have shelled out $2 million over the past five years to keep the Denver Broncos of the American Football League afloat, as saying, philanthropically, "It's our contribution to making Denver a complete city."

The third article, from *Business Week,* shifts the focus to hard-pressed country clubs which suddenly find their own revenues falling short of the (golfing) green and into the red. As some experts see it, only the wealthiest clubs can avoid being taxed out of business in the years ahead.

It is quite possible, that even the international Olympics —a sport of amateurs strictly dissociated from any taint of profit in the past—may ultimately be forced out of business by the high costs involved in putting on the show. An article from *U.S. News & World Report* shows how Sapporo, Japan, host to the 1972 Winter Games, rationalized the enormous expense involved by claiming it would have taken at least fifteen years to assemble the facilities generated on a crash basis. But, as the article points out, the people of Colorado, scheduled as hosts to the Winter Games in 1976, seemed reluctant to take on the honor, no matter what the ultimate gain in local improvements. And, in fact, in 1972, Coloradans voted to withdraw their bid for the Olympics, thereby demonstrating that costs and ecological considerations sometimes outweigh prestige.

In the final article in this section, a writer for *Business Week* sums up the financial difficulties facing many colleges and universities in their athletic programs today. Curiously, the article seems to debunk the old notion that good teams and fine athletes keep the money pouring in from the alumni. The money that does come in, it seems, is destined for sports programs themselves and has little impact on the academic needs of universities.

FINANCIAL WOES FOR PRO SPORTS [1]
Reprinted from *U.S. News & World Report.*

Professional sports are booming. Attendance has shot up 20 per cent in five years, dollar receipts even more. The number of major-league teams has more than doubled in a decade.

And yet—

The days of big profits seem to be ending. In one sport after another it is becoming harder for owners to earn a profit. About half of all pro teams—even some winners— are losing money.

[1] From "Pro Sports: A Business Boom in Trouble." *U.S. News & World Report.* 71:56-8. Jl. 5, '71.

Reasons: Costs are soaring even faster than incomes. Salaries of athletes are skyrocketing. Pro basketball, for example, finds its zooming gate receipts pouring out into million-dollar contracts for players. Other expenses—for travel, equipment, stadiums—also keep going up.

Inflation, in other words, has hit sports as it has other businesses.

As ticket prices are raised in attempts to keep pace with costs, thousands and thousands of spectators are being priced out of an expanding market.

Now even television revenues—which fueled the financial boom in sports—appear to have reached their peak.

As an investment, a team often produces a lower rate of return than a normal business.

Example: The Baltimore Orioles won the baseball championship of the American League and the World Series. Yet the Orioles netted only $345,000 after taxes on a gross income of $6.46 million—a rate of about 5 per cent. And that is believed to be the highest profit in the entire American League.

"From a financial point of view, some owners would be smarter to put their money into municipal bonds," says Harry Dalton, director of player personnel for the Orioles.

Still the cost of a sports franchise keeps rising. Even losers find buyers.

The explanation: There are many side benefits and compensations—such as the fun and glamour of running a big-league team, and the tax benefits available. Losses often can be written off against the owner's profits from another business. Ballplayers can be amortized as depreciable property. For example, a player costing $500,000 can be depreciated at the rate of $50,000 a year for ten years—the expectable length of his playing career.

For the financial picture of sports, the Economic Unit of *U.S. News & World Report* made a study of the major fields of competition. The results:

Of 24 major-league baseball teams, at least 1—and possibly 12—lost money last year [1970]. This was in spite of record attendance, up 27 per cent since 1965.

Seven of the known money losers were in the American League. Only three were in the National League, which outdrew the American by 4.5 million spectators.

Baseball officials say a club's profits can soar once its attendance passes 1.5 million a year. The Cincinnati Reds, for example, are reported to have made $2.5 million with 1.8 million attendance last year. The New York Mets made even more with 2.7 million.

The San Francisco Giants, on the other hand, reported a loss of $926,413 last season with 741,000 attendance.

Rising salaries are a problem. At least fifteen players now draw $100,000 a year or more. Three are on the Giants —including Willie Mays, who may top them all at $165,000.

Many executives say the upward salary trend jeopardizes the financial structure of the game. But Robert Howsam, Cincinnati general manager, notes:

"Although salaries are high, they amount to only 25 to 30 per cent of the total cost of running this ball club."

A major—and growing—cost is that of developing ballplayers. Bob Scheffing, general manager of the New York Mets, estimates that it costs $250,000 from the time a young player is signed until he is ready for the big leagues. Many a promising rookie paid a bonus to sign never makes the grade.

Major-league clubs spend, on the average, at least one million a year on minor-league operations to train players.

The total cost of operating a major-league baseball team is estimated to average $4.5 million to $5 million yearly.

Television is an important part of baseball income. Under a national contract providing $72 million over four years, each major-league club will get about $385,000. In addition, teams collect sums ranging from $400,000 to $1.8 million from local TV and radio. Without this broadcasting revenue, few teams would make profits.

Football: All Teams "in the Black"

Financially, football is the healthiest of all pro sports in the United States.

In 1970, attendance at all games hit 13.5 million for the 26 major-league teams. This was up 7.2 million from the 1965 total for 22 teams.

Football also earns more than $40 million a year from a national television package that is split among all teams —about $1.5 million each.

Football's gross revenue was estimated at $110 million . . . [in 1970], and no team is believed to have lost money.

The average net earnings per team were estimated at $600,000, with such well-established big-city teams as the New York Giants and Los Angeles Rams admitting profits above $1 million.

Yet football-team owners are worried. Privately they admit football may have reached its saturation point on TV. And with many teams playing to capacity crowds, there is little room for growth in attendance. Wellington Mara, owner of the New York Giants, says:

"The only way the Giants can make more revenue is by increasing ticket prices or getting more TV dollars. We are reluctant to do the former—and the latter just isn't going to happen."

Football salaries are high—and rising. A Giant spokesman says his club's payroll went up 50 per cent in the last five years. Another veteran-laden team reports its salary bill is in the area of $1.5 million. The average player earns $25,000 to $30,000 for the regular season—plus some $6,000 in fringe benefits and pay for preseason games. Some stars earn well above $100,000 a year.

Since a 1966 merger agreement ended a costly bidding war between the American and National leagues for talent, salaries have risen more slowly in football than in most other team sports. Now, according to Dan Rooney, general manager of the Pittsburgh Steelers: "Inflation is our No. 1 problem."

The richest bonanza in football has been the rapid growth in the value of a team. For example, the Philadelphia Eagles, bought for $5.5 million in 1963, sold for $16 million in 1969.

Few football owners foresee such a fast appreciation of their property in the next few years, however.

Basketball: Biggest Money Loser

Of all team sports, basketball is having the worst financial problems. Only 3 out of 28 teams in the two big leagues are believed operating at a profit.

The main reason, according to team owners and officials, is the high pay scale that has resulted from the war between the rival leagues—the American and National Basketball associations.

Freddy Schaus, general manager of the Los Angeles Lakers, estimates that the average salary, including "fringes," of a basketball player is about $50,000 a year— the highest in all professional team-sports. Superstars earn $150,000 or more yearly—several on long-term, million-dollar contracts. Lew Alcindor [now called Kareem Abdul-Jabbar], 7-foot, 2-inch center of the champion Milwaukee Bucks, is reputed to make about $250,000 a year.

"The supersalaries now being paid are hurting basketball," says Don De Jardin, general manager of the Philadelphia 76ers. "If they continue, a number of franchises will fold."

Although total attendance has zoomed, the number of teams sharing the spectators has increased from 8 to 28. And basketball can seat only a fraction of the crowds handled outdoors.

The New York Knickerbockers, with the NBA's largest attendance—18,622 per game—and a rich radio and TV market, are reported to have grossed about $6 million and netted more than $3 million last season.

Milwaukee's Bucks played to 99 per cent of their seating capacity, but grossed only about $2.8 million, with profits estimated at $300,000.

Only five NBA teams averaged more than nine thousand spectators per game—considered the minimum for a profit.

TV revenue is small, compared with football's. Each NBA team collects about $315,000 yearly from national telecasts. Most get $100,000 or more additional from local TV and radio.

Hockey: Profitable and Growing

In . . . [the years from 1966 to 1971] the National Hockey League has expanded from 6 teams to 14, and attendance has more than doubled—from 3.1 to nearly 8 million in the season just ended [1971].

Only three NHL teams are believed to have lost money last season.

Still, hockey has a problem: It has not caught on big over national television. The NHL got only about one million TV dollars last season.

Weston W. Adams, Jr., owner of the Boston Bruins, points out that six teams—including his own—sold out all seats at every game, so there is no room for attendance growth. He adds:

"Salaries have more than doubled in five years, and the players want more. The only way I see to increase revenue is to win a large national TV contract."

The average hockey player earns about $35,000 a year.

Golf, Racing and Bowling—All Growing

"Professional golf has grown financially by leaps and bounds," says Joseph C. Dey, Jr., commissioner of the tournament players' division of the Professional Golfers' Association (PGA). "We now have 350 professionals on the tour, playing in 63 events."

At least 16 golfers won more than $100,000 in 1970. In 1965 there were only two making that much money.

"Unlike other sports, golf-tournament organizers are not in the business to coin money," says one promoter. "The only persons who profit in a golf tournament are the players themselves."

Horse racing and dog racing drew more spectators than any other sport—79.6 million total last year.

Betting—the lifeblood of racing—exceeded $6.5 billion, which was far above the amount spent on any other professional sport.

States permitting parimutuel betting at tracks collected more than $525 million in taxes. Now off-track betting has been legalized in New York, and other states may follow.

Auto racing now ranks second only to animal racing as a spectator sport. And prizes get bigger every year.

"A driver who not long ago raced on Sunday for a $10 trophy now is a businessman who grosses $100,000 a year," says W. Richard Smith, a vice president of a new $20 million track at Ontario, California.

Once dominated by the long races such as the Indianapolis 500, this sport now offers a wide variety of events, including stock-car races and the fast-growing sanctioned drag races. At least a dozen dragsters take in $150,000 or more a year.

Of racing's 42 million spectators in 1970, between 8 and 10 million attended drag races.

A car race is a complex commercial event, with many business firms contributing to the big purses as a way of advertising their products.

Professional bowling began little more than a decade ago, but some 32 or more tournaments will pay nearly $2 million in prizes this year. Johnny Petraglia already

—at midseason—has topped the previous record of $67,375 for earnings in a year.

TROUBLE FOR THE FRONT OFFICE [2]

The Oakland Athletics baseball team seems to have a lot going for it. The club has been in the thick of the American League's Western Division pennant race for much of the season [1969]. It has a new 50,000-seat stadium and a young slugger named Reggie Jackson who has a chance to set a major-league home-run record. [He didn't. —Ed.] Yet unless attendance picks up appreciably, the A's stand to wind up the year losing money.

Owner Charles O. Finley, who moved the A's from Kansas City in 1968, thinks things will straighten themselves out "as soon as we establish ourselves in Oakland." Others, however, see it differently. They say Mr. Finley might have erred in bringing the team to a city that has been known as a "tough" box-office town since vaudeville days. More generally, "The A's are one of the worst-run outfits around," says a close observer of the team's affairs. "If Finley ran his insurance business like he runs his ball club, he'd be broke in a week."

The specific reasons for the flounderings of the A's might be unique, but their financial plight isn't. Contrary to public belief, many professional sports teams have proved to be less than a bonanza for their owners, even in these days of juicy television contracts and widespread interest in sports.

Big-league baseball, for instance, is enjoying something of a revival this year [1969], but at least 9 of its 24 teams seems likely to finish the campaign in the red. The National Basketball Association set an attendance record last season, but 7 of its 14 members say they lost money. Four of

[2] From "The Front Office: Owning a Sports Team Looks Like Fun, But It Isn't Always Gold Mine," by Frederick C. Klein, staff reporter. *Wall Street Journal.* 174:1+. S. 9, '69. Reprinted by permission.

the American Football League's 10 teams were financial losers in 1968, as were 2 of 12 National Hockey League clubs. The National Football League is pro sports' most profitable league, but even there several teams are said to be operating close to the break-even point.

Owners are quick to blame their problems on fast-rising costs—especially players' salaries—but that's not the whole story, some observers assert.

"The fact is that some—maybe most—sports franchises aren't especially well managed," says Bill Veeck, who at various times owned the baseball Chicago White Sox, Cleveland Indians and St. Louis Browns and now is president of Suffolk Downs Race Track near Boston. He adds: "Sensible, successful businessmen have been known to change once they become club owners. They do things they wouldn't dream of doing with the businesses that made them successful." Among the common foibles of sports owners are nepotism, interference with coaches even though they lack expertise and a tendency to use their teams as a means of boosting their egos rather than making money.

Some pro teams are quite well-run, of course. The baseball Los Angeles Dodgers, Houston Astros and New York Yankees get generally high marks, as do the football Dallas Cowboys and Cleveland Browns and the NBA [National Basketball Association] Milwaukee Bucks and Philadelphia 76ers, among others.

No one is shedding too many tears for the rest because pro team ownership contains fringe benefits that make it tough for even the least efficient owner to lose money in the long run. New owners can benefit from substantial depreciation write-offs, and owners of existing teams stand to split handsome bounties when their leagues admit new members, as they've done frequently of late. Enough rich sportsmen are interested in having a pro team of their own to keep pushing up the resale value of franchises.

A Skeptical View

Even the owners' claims of losses from daily operations are discounted by at least one individual who has dealt with many teams. He says the books of privately owned teams are "a no-man's land full of places where income can be hidden."

To team officials, though, the losses are all too real. "We're in a real predicament," says Joe L. Brown, Jr., general manager of the baseball Pittsburgh Pirates, who lost money last year and expects a similar result this year. "We've got to meet rising costs while keeping ticket prices at the workingman's level. If we tried to recoup our costs at the gate, we'd price ourselves right out of the market."

Costs aside, the motives of a good many team owners suggest maximum profit isn't their number one goal. Some, like Robert E. Short, a Minneapolis trucking-company owner who paid almost $10 million to buy the money-losing Washington Senators last year, are in sports mainly because the publicity aids their other enterprises. "Sports-page identification helps my trucking business so much that the Senators will be worth the price if they just manage to break even," Mr. Short says.

Gerald and Allan Phipps, two wealthy brothers, say that civic duty has led them to shell out some $2 million over the past five years to keep the AFL [American Football League] Denver Broncos afloat. "It's our contribution to making Denver a complete city," says Allan, a lawyer. He believes a pro football team "is as necessary to a community as libraries, museums and a symphony orchestra."

Bill Veeck says that "ego satisfaction" plays a big role with some club owners. They "like the prestige of associating with athletes and being on the inside of all the strategy talk before the big game," he contends.

Apparently in that category is Daniel E. Reeves, a millionaire former stockbroker who owns the NFL [National Football League] Los Angeles Rams. Mr. Reeves fired head coach George Allen after last season, despite the fact that over Mr. Allen's three-year tenure the team had an excellent 30-win, 10-loss, 2-tie record and made a lot of money. Mr. Reeves later rehired Mr. Allen after exacting a promise that the coach would meet with him at least once a week.

"Dan was sore because George was so wrapped up in coaching he didn't have time to make small talk with him about football," says someone who is close to the Rams.

Some owners insist on taking an active hand in the on-field operations of their teams—frequently to the chagrin of their coaches or managers. One owner, husky, thirty-year-old John Mecom, Jr., of the NFL New Orleans Saints, keeps tab on things by regularly suiting up and working out with his team. *Sports Illustrated* magazine once commented that Saints' coach Tom Fears "cannot be expected to shiver with delight" at Mr. Mecom's custom.

The Oakland A's Mr. Finley is considered to be pro sports' most persistent owner-meddler. He fired seven managers while losing about $3 million in seven years at Kansas City, and he once even fired a player, slugger Ken Harrelson. From his Chicago insurance office or summer home in La Porte, Indiana, he continues to run the A's down to such minutiae as approving the ads for the team's daily score-card. "I do things the way I think they ought to be done," says Mr. Finley.

The Athletics' owner has a couple of rivals in the NBA: Fred Zollner of the Detroit Pistons and Dick Klein of the Chicago Bulls. Mr. Zollner, who also owns a company that makes pistons, has employed a half-dozen coaches in as many seasons. "His three-year rebuilding programs usually last about a year," says a former Piston. Mr. Zollner hasn't been available for comment on his policies.

A Long-Term Contract

Mr. Klein, who made his money running a sales-promotion firm, . . . sold a player [in 1968] without telling his coach,

Dick Motta. This led the short-handed Mr. Motta to threaten to throw a dollar bill onto the court to see how it played. Mr. Klein was removed as the Bulls' general manager two weeks ago, though he remains a part-owner of the team. In defense of his trading actions, Mr. Klein has said that "there often are factors the occasional fan has no knowledge of."

At the other extreme are owners who give their coaches too much security. The . . . owner of the NFL Philadelphia Eagles will have to pay Joe Kuharich $49,000 a year . . . [until 1980] unless the recently fired Eagles coach gets a new job; the team's previous owner had given Mr. Kuharich a fifteen-year contract. Mr. Kuharich was the object of a spirited "Joe Must Go" campaign that helped Eagles fans enliven an otherwise gloomy season . . . [in 1968] (the Eagles lost their first eleven games and ended the season with twelve losses and two wins).

Front-office operations of many teams would give a management consultant nightmares. When CBS bought the New York Yankees from millionaire sportsmen Dan Topping and Del Webb in 1965, it found the eighty-member office force could easily be trimmed by about a dozen, according to Michael Burke, whom CBS installed as the Yanks' president. Mr. Burke estimates that the team's administrative costs are now about 25 percent lower than before the takeover.

Even though pro teams are sizable enterprises with revenues that run as high as $7 million a year, the big majority continue to approach the hiring of front-office personnel on a strictly informal basis. Few clubs do any recruiting; most owners prefer to apportion jobs among relatives, friends or people who just happen to present themselves. "Why should we recruit?" asks owner Ralph Wilson of the AFL Buffalo Bills. "Just about every day we get letters from people who'd love to work for a pro football team."

Pro sports' champion practitioner of nepotism is Minnesota Twins' owner Calvin Griffith, whose son, sister, three brothers and a nephew all hold executive-level jobs with his baseball team. [Calvin Griffith, whose original name was Robertson, was adopted by Clark Griffith, late owner of the Washington Senators.—Ed.] Earlier this season, Twins' manager Billy Martin publicly suggested that Mr. Griffith's brother Sherrard Robertson, vice president in charge of farm teams, didn't know his business too well. Mr. Martin took exception to a Robertson decision to drop a pitcher who almost made the Twins to a low-level farm team instead of to the Twins' Triple A affiliate in Denver, the level immediately below the majors. "If he's almost good enough to pitch for us, he ought to be good enough to pitch for Denver," the manager said.

"I don't tell Martin how to manage, and I don't need him to tell me how to run the farm department," Mr. Robertson retorted.

To some sports executives, all talk about front-office efficiency is beside the point. They assert that the sole factor in financial success is a winning team on the field and that their main job is to keep their players happy. But insurance man Sidney Salomon, Jr., ran into criticism from fellow owners when he tried to follow this advice after buying the St. Louis franchise in the 1967 NHL [National Hockey League] expansion.

Mr. Salomon's practice of treating his players and their wives to free vacations at his Florida hotel and rewarding exceptional performances with bonus gifts put him on "very thin ice," one NHL executive was quoted as saying. He explained that soon other teams' players might start expecting the same treatment.

"The idea of incentives for players is ridiculous," agrees a top baseball executive. "A man making $100,000 a year shouldn't have to be bribed to play well." (Actually, big-league baseball salaries average around $25,000.)

But players sometimes grumble that some teams are less than generous in certain things. Associations that represent pro athletes in fringe-benefit negotiations with owners complain that it hasn't been uncommon for teams to schedule road trips so that players don't get their full day's meal allowances. The Pittsburgh Pirates have purchased team blazers for their players to wear on the road, but when one tried to get some extra use from his by wearing his handkerchief so that it covered the team name on the pocket, he was ordered to sew the pocket shut.

FALLING SHORT OF THE GREEN [3]

The River Oaks Country Club is probably the most exclusive golf club in Houston. Membership runs to old money (by Texas standards), and the old ways change slowly. But changes are coming this year [1971]. River Oaks will hit its members with a 5-10 percent dues increase, the first in seventeen years; greens fees for guests will climb 30 percent; locker rents will go up; and dishwashing machines will help automate the club's food services. Such steps are necessary, says club manager Willard "Red" Steger, because labor costs are soaring, and because members have been spending less time and money at the club because of the stock-market slump.

But River Oaks' problems are mild compared to the financial squeeze on many of the other 4,600-odd private golf clubs in the United States. The squeeze is tightest in the Northeast and Midwest, where the recession has hit harder and golfers are just now starting to loosen swings after the winter layoff:

In Watertown, Massachusetts, the Oakley Country Club had to impose two special assessments on members to stay in the black after they voted down a dues increase and rejected a real-estate developer's offer to buy the golf course for $5 million.

[3] From "Country Clubs Fall Short of the Green." *Business Week.* p 77-8. Mr. 6, '71. Reprinted from the March 6, 1971 issue of *Business Week* by special permission. Copyrighted © 1971 by McGraw-Hill, Inc.

In Cleveland, many golf clubs have been "on the brink of disaster" in the past year [1970], according to Henry Meiers, president of the Cleveland District Golf Association. The situation has eased a bit lately, partly because repeal of some Ohio blue laws has permitted country clubs to serve beverages more potent than 3.2 beer on Sundays. But, adds Meiers, "If this recession had gone further, there could have been clubs going out of business."

One very prestigious club in New York's Westchester suburbs had its property tax hiked by 40 percent after three years of wage inflation had boosted operating costs by 62 percent. Though the $960 yearly dues were already well above average, it had to hike them to $1,800 for 1971 and cut back services. This was too much even for this club's affluent members: the manager reports that 10 percent of them have resigned.

Like many other club officials, the Westchester man would discuss his troubles only after assurance that he would not be identified. In a world that prizes privacy as much as exclusivity, club finances are a sensitive subject. "We should have a membership drive tomorrow," says the manager of a country club outside Atlanta. "In the North it's acceptable, but in the South it just isn't done. If we started going after new members, people would say, 'What in the world is wrong with them? They must be going broke.' "

But the situation is revealed clearly enough in a survey of seventy-five country clubs by Harris, Kerr, Forster & Company, an accounting firm that specializes in club finances. The survey shows that clubs' average operating costs climbed 10.4 percent in 1970, reflecting the inflation in everything from bartenders' wages to the price of the bent-grass seed used on greens. Rent, taxes, and other fixed costs rose 9.5 percent partly because of tougher regulation by the Internal Revenue Service of nonprofit clubs' tax exemptions and pressures from local authorities who see expanses of fairway as a tempting source of new tax revenues.

Just as costs have begun to rise steeply, the recession has cut into the restaurant and bar business, golf cart rentals, and other income clubs rely on to fill the gap between dues and expenses. Besides impelling members to pare personal spending, the slowdown has moved corporations to tighten reins on executives with company-paid memberships—the sales types who are accustomed to mix business with golf and associated wassail. A Houston club manager reports he had to cancel "a very large cocktail party" recently after the local affiliate of a New York Company got orders to cut costs.

"Clubs are luxuries, and when budgets are tight, clubs are the first to go," says Irvin Kingsley, manager of the Bel Air Country Club in Los Angeles. "In these times, a man is more likely to go home than to the club after work." Kingsley, who is a national director of the Club Managers Association of America, says that waiting lists for admission to membership rolls, which used to run from two to five years for first-rate clubs, are now down to less than a single year for most of the United States.

All this has chopped a sizable divot out of income. Despite dues increases that averaged 6 percent in the Harris, Kerr, Forster survey, the decline in clubs' operating income last year made a 36 percent dent in balances available for paying off debt and for capital improvements.

Out of the Trap

Clubs have been forced into all sorts of maneuvers to make ends meet. Some have levied special assessments on members. Others, like the Innis Arden Golf Club in Old Greenwich, Connecticut, have set minimum charges to force members to spend more time and money at the club. Innis Arden's $100-per-quarter minimum reportedly is stimulating business considerably just before each three-month deadline, as members flock to the restaurant and bar to spend the money they would be assessed in any case.

At the famous Winged Foot Golf Club in Mamaroneck, New York, where a union contract raised greenskeepers' pay by 35 percent and a new school levy added $35,000 to the annual tax bill this year, dues and the initiation fee have been raised by $100 each. In addition, manager Gerald Healy plans to operate with 24 greenskeepers instead of 28 this year by adding more power mowers. He will also make Tuesdays "lunch only" days, eliminating the six-day week and the time-and-a-half pay restaurant employees collect for the sixth day.

Most clubs try to ease the burden on dues-payers by occasionally opening clubhouses and courses to nonmembers for charity balls, golf tournaments, and other income-producing events. But the IRS [Internal Revenue Service] of late has been taking a stern view of moneymaking activities by nonprofit clubs.

A 1964 tax law ruled that a nonprofit club could derive no more than 5 percent of its income from nonmember functions—as opposed to income from "members and bona fide guests"—without losing tax-exempt status. On top of that, the 1969 tax reform act taxed such "nonrelated income" at corporate rates.

The impact of these laws is still uncertain. "We've been waiting seven years for the IRS to decide what constitutes a 'bona fide guest,'" says Arthur Iredell, senior partner in Harris, Kerr, Forster. Among other things, Iredell notes, the IRS has yet to rule how clubs should allocate overhead and other expenses in computing net taxable income. But club managers are taking no chances. Most are holding nonmember functions to a minimum.

River Oaks manager Red Steger says he is especially concerned that clubs may be taxed on any income from members who are reimbursed by their companies. The IRS is considering this on the ground that companies deduct such perquisites as expense-account golf in figuring their own taxable income. And legal counsel Jack Janetatos of the National Club Association [NCA] is convinced that the threat is serious. "I suggest strongly that every [tax-exempt] club make certain that the only checks it receives from members are their personal checks—not company checks made out to the club or made out to members and turned over to the club," Janetatos told an NCA tax clinic recently.

Local Hazards

If the country-club life is under assault from Washington, it faces an even greater threat closer to home. New York State has levied a 7 percent tax on "nonrelated" income, and Connecticut has imposed a 10 percent excise tax on club dues. Town and county governments all over suburbia are raising the low-tax assessments traditionally given to golf clubs as "green-belt benefits." Some two-hundred-acre golf courses formerly assessed as farmland have been revalued on the basis of "best potential use"—an expensive change in areas deemed suitable for housing developments or high-rise apartments. The St. Clair Club outside Pittsburgh, for example, had its assessment boosted to $1.4 million from $440,000 last year [1970], raising its annual tax bill $70,000. Like dozens of clubs in a similar fix, St. Clair is appealing to the courts.

"There is a lot of pressure on clubs to sell out and move to lower-tax areas," says consultant Iredell. "We in the club industry feel it is desirable to maintain these areas for ecology reasons."

For local authorities facing problems of population growth and revenue shortages, ecological arguments for open spaces restricted to members only are not always convincing. Consumerist Ralph Nader has taken on the issue in Maryland, one of the few states where green-belt benefits are a matter of state policy. In a letter to Governor Marvin Mandel, Nader asserted that the public was losing $160,000 in revenue in Montgomery County by subsidizing private golf clubs. "If they can't afford to keep land close in [to Washington, D.C.], why shouldn't they be forced to sell out?" asked Nader.

Some clubmen feel that in the long run only the wealthiest clubs can avoid being taxed out of business. As for building new golf courses, Desmond Muirhead, a top golf-architect, says: "To make economic sense, new courses should be associated with resort hotels or real estate developments."

THE COSTLY WORLD OF THE OLYMPICS [4]

Reprinted from *U.S. News & World Report.*

Here is a facet of the Olympic Games generally overlooked by athletes and sports enthusiast around the world—

Japan is spending more than half a billion dollars to host this year's [1972] Winter Games, which opened February 3.

Only a small part of this cost will be recovered by sale of 800,000 tickets and from spending by the thousands of visitors jamming this mountain-rimmed city on Hokkaido, Japan's northernmost island. Much of the cost will come out of the taxpayers' pockets. This question is raised:

Are the Olympic games worth their cost to the people who foot the bill?

Most Japanese appear to think so. The Olympic spending is generally regarded . . . as a good investment with a double payoff: lavish new public works for Sapporo and its surrounding territory, plus added prestige for this area and the nation as a whole.

Referring to the highways, subway, housing and other facilities that have been constructed in preparation for the Olympics, Mayor Takeshi Itagaki said:

"Without the Olympics, it would have taken Sapporo at least fifteen years longer to acquire these facilities—and some of them, such as the subway, we might never have gotten."

[4] From "Does It Pay to Be Host to Olympics?" *U.S. News & World Report.* 72:60-1. F. 14, '72.

Not so confident of the Olympics' economic value, however, are some citizens of Colorado, where the 1976 Winter Games... [were] to be held.

A delegation of Coloradans came . . . [to Sapporo] to protest to the International Olympic Committee against the spending that . . . [would] be imposed upon their state and to ask that the next Winter Games be moved elsewhere.

"We feel Colorado should not be spending hundreds of millions of dollars on staging the Oympics when we don't have adequate schools, health facilities, police protection and environmental control," said Mrs. Estelle Brown of Denver, who led the protesting delegation. She predicted the Olympic construction and crowds would damage the mountain environment near Denver.

The Denver Olympic Committee, however, . . . claimed 70 percent of all Coloradans in favor of hosting the games. And no move was made by the International Olympic Committee to abandon the Denver site. [In November 1972 a Colorado bond issue to finance the games was defeated. Later, Innsbruck, Austria was chosen as the site of the 1976 games.—Ed.]

Squaw Valley, California, was the last American site for the Winter Olympics. That was in 1960. There are still arguments about whether that venture paid off. But according to California park officials, the general feeling is that the state got its money's worth.

Grenoble, France, which hosted the Winter Olympics of 1968, also appears to be generally satisfied with the economic results.

Here in Sapporo, the prevailing atmosphere is one of high optimism.

Preparation for the Olympics has created a building and employment boom. In each of the last five years [1967-1971], spending in connection with the games has amounted to roughly half of all new capital investment here. The demand for labor has contributed to a 200,000 increase in the area's population and a 20 percent hike in wages—accompanied by rising consumer prices.

Only about $58 million was spent directly on sports facilities—such as a speed-skating rink with seats for 46,000 people, a 90-meter ski jump and a bobsled run. But nearly ten times that amount was poured into projects related to the Olympics.

It is out of these related projects that the Hokkaido area expects to reap much future benefit.

Highway and Village

A new highway has been built linking Sapporo with the international airport at Chitose, an hour's bus ride away.

The initial leg has been built on the first subway in Sapporo, a city of one million population. The rubber-tired subway trains run from Sapporo to the Olympic Village, where some 1,100 athletes from thirty-five nations are housed.

The newly built Olympic Village is Japan's first large apartment complex with a central heating system. After the games, the apartments will be sold to Japanese families at prices from $16,000 to $32,000 per apartment.

To handle the hoped-for shopping boom from Olympic visitors, private investors underwrote construction of stores, hotels, and an underground shopping center.

Other improvements include fifty miles of sewage and drainage pipes, new parks and added airport facilities.

All these are expected to be useful long after the games. Twelve of the 14 sites built for Olympic competition also will be retained. Local boosters hope to see Sapporo become an international winter-sports capital.

There is little hope of maintaining the boom of the last five years. A post-Olympic slump and a rise in unemployment are considered inevitable. The hope is that any short-term setbacks will be offset by long-range benefits.

Plans call for future expansion of the new subway and for building additional miles of express highways. Construction of two department stores and at least four hotels is due to begin next year.

Sapporo—unknown to most foreigners in the past—is now on the world map. And citizens . . . cannot understand the misgivings of some Coloradans.

Says Kenji Sato, a Sapporo businessman: "In another fifty years, when our public-works projects have become outmoded, it will be time for Sapporo to host another Winter Olympics."

Commercialism and the Future of the Olympics

It may be, however, that the Winter Olympics will not be continued very many years into the future—at least in their present form.

This possibility was voiced . . . on January 30 [1972] by Avery Brundage, the eighty-four-year-old American who for years has been president of the International Olympic Committee. Lamenting the rising costs and increasing commercialism of the Winter Games, he predicted that they "will find it hard to continue as an amateur event." [Avery Brundage has since retired.—Ed.]

Mr. Brundage had attempted to bar a number of European skiers from competing here on charges of professionalism, maintaining that they had let their names and pictures be used for advertisement of ski gear.

There were threats of withdrawal by ski teams of several nations if any of their stars were banned. Eventually, only one skier was ruled out: Karl Schranz of Austria. And, at his request, the Austrian team did not withdraw.

The games were saved—for this year [1972]. But the clouds of commercialism, economic risk and doubt still hung menacingly over the future of the Winter Olympic Games.

COLLEGE SPORTS FACE FINANCIAL SQUEEZE [5]

The long football tradition began in 1894 at the State University of New York at Buffalo [then the University of Buffalo]. Down the years, players would be summoned to practice in these waning weeks of summer. But this year [1971], a fading athletics budget has blown the final whistle on football at the 24,000-student university.

The same thing has happened at eighteen other schools in just the past five years, with more to come. The sports programs at more than 400 of the 655 schools that make up the National Collegiate Athletic Association [NCAA] are in the red. The schools of the Ivy League, the Big Ten, and the Big Eight, which often spend more than $3 million a year on their programs, are suffering, too—one third of them have an average annual deficit of $176,000; up 110 percent in the last ten years. [There are eight Ivy League teams: Brown, Columbia, Cornell, Dartmouth, Harvard, Pennsylvania, Princeton, Yale. The Big Eight consists of Colorado, Iowa State, Kansas State, Kansas, Missouri, Nebraska, Oklahoma, Oklahoma State. The Big Ten is made up of Illinois, Indiana, Iowa, Michigan State, Michigan, Minnesota, Northwestern, Ohio State, Purdue, Wisconsin.] Even Ohio State, which has already had to turn away more than five thousand late applicants for season football tickets to its 80,000-seat stadium, will just meet its $3.7 million athletics budget this year.

To survive, schools are cutting their sports budgets. Yale, for one, has lopped off 10 percent. Another tack, taken by Pennsylvania, Wisconsin, Yale, and others, is to drop freshman teams in the nonrevenue sports, which include just about everything except football and basketball.

Cutbacks come as a shock in places where football is a religion, such as Alabama where there are more alumni willing to shell out $1,500 for sports scholarships than there are

[5] From "College Sports Feel Budget Ax." *Business Week.* p 38-9. Ag. 28, '71. Reprinted from the August 28, 1971 issue of *Business Week* by special permission. Copyrighted © 1971 by McGraw-Hill, Inc.

scholarships available. Still, Alabama is "tightening up over-all," and the athletic department went so far as to eliminate the annual shrimp supper it hosts for high school coaches.

The cutting list is long: Princeton has eliminated its training table at lunch, Rutgers discourages guests at its table, Stanford has decided not to fill vacancies in the coaching staffs, and Illinois is not replacing team uniforms as frequently as it used to. Travel is another target: Harvard is busing its teams to Princeton instead of flying and cuts out overnight trips; Penn is trying to schedule two teams on one bus; and schools generally go the most inexpensive route, avoiding long trips and hotel bills.

Recruiting is another expense that has gone under the knife. Missouri, like Illinois, has cut out what it calls "extravagance." Harvard coaches have been relieved of the costly "ordeal-by-rubber-chicken" recruiting circuit. Purchasing departments have also gotten the word, and at Wisconsin, for one, there is now more care taken in buying equipment, while at Cincinnati they are saving on the laundry. All these measures still have not yet been enough to stem the tide of sports spending in the colleges, which in the last decade has risen 108 percent (only one third of that due to inflation).

The Breakdown

Program expansion accounts for a fourth of the increase, but the rest—and the real sore spot—includes what Oregon State's athletic director, Jim Barett, calls "keeping up with the Joneses." What this means is hiring extra coaches, traveling by air (first class), arriving at games a day early to "acclimatize" the players, and other such amenities.

At the same time, the fundamental costs of an ongoing sports program are difficult to whittle down. And the costs of grants-in-aid are no mean sum. A "full-ride" grant covers tuition, room and board, fees, books, and spending money. At Tennessee, these grants run to 40 percent of all scholarships; at Alabama, they total 45 percent, or $400,000.

While costs escalate, student support in some places is dwindling. For one thing, students have been voting to withhold fees that go to intercollegiate sports. It has happened at small Whittier and large Kansas, and such a vote could cost California at Berkeley $400,000. An Illinois spokesman says that because the school does not collect such a fee, "we don't have the extra luxury some schools do."

Actually, what Illinois needs most right now is a winning football team. Like all schools, it finds that the budget totals "depend on what happens in football," which often pays the freight for a school's athletics program. For example, Southern California, which usually fields winning teams in many sports, took in $1.6 million last year over-all, $1 million of that from football, and the football revenue was enough to pay all costs. But at Miami losing eight football games meant a $170,000 deficit. The school has already dropped basketball, and if the football team does not improve, says President Henry Stanford, "we'll do some soul-searching."

Often, winning is not enough. Despite sellout crowds, Ohio State's assistant vice president, Ernest Leggett, says that expanding costs still hurt because "the stadium and the basketball arena are still the same size." And while Harvard's basketball team is first rate, it cannot pay its way, because it plays in a dilapidated, third-floor gym that seats only 1,600.

The Outlook

In the 1960s, television contracts helped ease the budget squeeze. But not much more help can be expected from them. ABC-TV last year [1970] lost $4.5 million on its NCAA deals. Besides, the NCAA ordinarily allows each school only three appearances in two years.

A reason often given for maintaining large sports programs is that sports will bring in alumni support to the general coffers, and Stanford's Rose Bowl victory is credited with taking old grads' minds off student disruptions. But it seems that sports buffs' money often goes just to sports, creating a $2.6 million athletic building for USC or paying much of the cost of Colorado's Astroturf. It builds stadiums, but USC for one, finds no correlation between winning in those stadiums and winning in the treasurer's office.

Still, most schools with an athletic tradition fear any cutbacks that could undermine their competitive position, so they limit their cost cutting to strictly minor-league measures. Even conference-wide rules that could produce savings in six figures meet stiff resistance. Few conferences have done more than just talk about limiting the size of the coaching staffs and the number of scholarships—the two major cost items in big-time college athletics.

The NCAA wants to limit recruiting, reduce the number of scholarships and limit them to those who need them, and cut back on coaching staffs. There is a lot of opposition in many big schools to tampering with their scholarship structure. Some schools threaten to walk out of the association even though a study shows that these measures could save them as much as $250,000. Walter Byers, NCAA president, says that if schools do not come up with a game plan to beat spiraling costs and standstill profits, they may be benched permanently. He says: "There is an economic morality, too, you know."

VI. REGULATION, REFORM, AND REDEMPTION

EDITOR'S INTRODUCTION

Americans spend $400 million a year on admissions to spectator sports, where the financial wrangling and uproar appear to be concentrated. But Americans also spend almost ten times as much on sports supplies and equipment for their own use. They spend ten times as much, also, on hunting and fishing licenses, equipment and related expenses. They spend more than twice as much just on building their own swimming pools and equipping them with accessories. Four hundred million dollars is a great deal of money, but it is a mere drop in the bucket compared to the total leisure-time spending of Americans today.

If any readers should be depressed about the commercialism of spectator sports in America today, therefore, let them consider the increasing move by Americans toward participation sports. Let them consider, as the final section of this compilation does, the reforms being generated in pro sports, the "civic" uses being found in such innovations as off-track betting on the horses, and the way Americans are shucking their roles as passive spectators to become activists and sportsmen in their own right and according to their own inclinations. And let them take heart. Far from being in the doldrums, sports in America today are enjoying their greatest popularity in history.

The first article in this section recounts the dazzling statistics regarding money spent on participation sports in 1972. The next article discusses congressional efforts, still underway, to accord a greater degree of free competition to professional sports than club owners have heretofore found practicable. The third article examines off-track betting as an economic and social step forward, while the final excerpt reports on the sums being spent on recreation, generally, in America today.

THE BOOM IN PARTICIPATION SPORTS [1]

Americans with increasing amounts of leisure sought pleasure in jogging, boating, tennis, skiing, golf, cycling, snorkeling, snowmobiling, riding, bowling, camping, pool, chess, backgammon and just plain relaxing in record numbers in 1972.

And 1973 promises to involve another record number of persons in recreational activities according to United Press International.

The leisure-time market now accounts for a total expenditure of $100 billion, more than the cost of national defense.

The pleasure-boat industry reported a 25 percent increase over 1971 boat sales. Some 45.5 million Americans have taken to the waterways in one form or another, some of them to live aboard luxuriously appointed houseboats.

The number of tennis players was up 20 percent, bicyclists 15 and skiers 10. Golf had only a 4 percent increase in players at the nation's 10,665 courses, 151 of them new. There are now 10.4 million regular golfers and 2.35 million who play 15 or fewer rounds a year.

A new sport, sky surfing, has just appeared on the California horizon and has at least three hundred enthusiasts. They jump off seacliffs and desert rockfaces tied to giant delta-wing kites originally designed for the evacuation of combat pilots. Sky-surfing equipment costs about $150.

At the sedentary end of the recreation spectrum, chess and backgammon are having a comeback that games-industry sources describe as "fantastic." Chess sets, ranging from $25 to $10,000 in price, can hardly be manufactured quickly enough to meet the demand since the widely publicized

[1] From "Americans Spent More Money and More Time Just Playing." New York *Times*. p 14 S. D. 31, '72. © 1972 by The New York Times Company. Reprinted by permission.

Bobby Fischer-Boris Spassky world championship match . . .
[in 1972]. Even Salvador Dali designed a set.

Backgammon, as old as King Tut but pretty much relegated to high-society resorts since an era of popularity in the
twenties, is booming because more city dwellers are staying
indoors at night. Most good players play for money and
tournaments have sprung up from New York to Las Vegas.
Investment in a set can range from $10 to $975 for a leather-
bound arrangement.

The most controversial of new sports, snowmobiling, is
noisy, dangerous and tempting to drivers with trespass ten-
dencies.

In the 1968-69 winter season there were 54 snowmobile
fatalities nationally and in succeeding seasons the figure
rose to 84, 104, and 164. . . . There are 1.25 million registered snowmobiles.

Americans purchased 700,000 boats in 1972, 400,00 of
them power boats. Rowboats and canoes accounted for
200,000 of the total. So crowded are American waters by
nine million boats that resulting pollution has forced pas-
sage of Federal legislation to require holding tanks for
waste for later onshore disposal. Boats built after January 1,
1973, must have this equipment. Installation in older
registered pleasure boats must be made within a few years.

Tennis is a $420 million business with all-weather court
enclosures accounting for an increasing slice of the gross.
Pre-engineering has brought the cost down to $250,000 and
delivery takes only a few weeks. There are seven hundred
such courts nationwide and the figure is growing at the
rate of one a day.

Skiing is a billion-dollar industry with half the money
going into transportation to and from the nation's 1,200
developed slope resorts.

There were 50,000 leg breaks last season [1971-1972], but
plastic boots, fiberglass skis and mechanical antifriction

devices already have made a dent in the injury rate that held at four for [each] 1,000 skiers for years.

Bicycles are tooling along in greater numbers. Sales [were] 10.5 million in 1972, about equaling the sale of automobiles. The owners of the nation's 75 million two-wheelers form a powerful lobby and have been successful in getting bike traffic lanes and trails, safe parking facilities and safety regulations in many areas.

California has a statewide network of bike trails and Oregon is spending one cent of every highway dollar on cycling needs.

The ten-speed bike is king of the road, and the manufacturers can't turn them out fast enough. There even are bicycles built for three. These superior vehicles have a resale value of $70 and up, and thieves are not unaware of this. They steal millions of dollars' worth of bikes a year —$22.3 million in California alone in 1971.

Motorcycles, which represent an investment of at least $250, are selling at an "unbelievable" rate, according to industry sources. There are 3.8 million registered motorcycles in private hands.

Travel trailers, of which 62,600 were produced in 1961, have given birth to a family of camping vehicles—camping trailers, truck campers, pickup covers and motor homes. Production has risen to over 549,000 annually for total sales of more than $1.7 billion. Motor homes with complete living facilities, priced from $5,000 to $20,000, are a fast-moving item.

Snorkeling is overtaking water-skiing as a top aquatic sport.

And pool tables may soon outnumber pianos in American homes. The cost of warp-proof, slate-bed billiard tables has been cut to as little as $350 and the game has the advantage of costing no money after the original investment.

REGULATING THE PROS [2]

"Apparently the only criterion for measuring success in baseball these days is the profit-and-loss statement on the books, not the win-loss column in the daily newspaper."

Thus, fulminated Democratic Representative B. F. Sisk, among others, in the removal of Washington's baseball Senators to Texas. The team owner's search for a more lucrative market was a harsh reminder to the California Congressman and other shattered Senators fans that professional sport is a business.

But free enterprise it is not, at least not completely. Both law and custom allow monopolistic conspiracies in restraint of the trade of selling tickets to people who want to see indentured athletes perform. When the system somehow angers outsiders like Representative Sisk, the demands for reform go in opposite directions: (1) Either bring more free enterprise to the sports business by making team owners compete harder for ticket buyers and players; or (2) If the business is a monopoly anyway, push it completely to the status of a public utility, with regulation of ticket prices, players' contracts, territories and rates of return.

The question of new business ground rules for professional sport may be coming to a climax in Congress, and not just because the capital has lost its baseball team. At immediate issue is legislation allowing a merger of the two major professional basketball leagues. That bill is important in its own right, but it's also becoming the vehicle for a sweeping re-examination of the laws affecting baseball and football. The basketball merger bill, says California's Democratic Senator John Tunney, "has opened up the subject of sports and the antitrust laws in a way that the subject has never been opened up before."

[2] From "Blowing the Whistle on Pro Sports," by Arlen J. Large, a member of *The Wall Street Journal*'s Washington Bureau. *Wall Street Journal.* p 20. O. 20, '71. Reprinted by permission.

One reason for expecting fireworks in the months ahead is that an influential Senator named Sam Ervin has his back up about "the evils of the big sports monopolies." The North Carolina Democrat is acting chairman of the Senate Antitrust subcommittee that . . . [has conducted] hearings on the basketball bill. . . . [Various bills are still under consideration.—Ed.] Senator Ervin wants to kill the basketball bill, but if he can't, he has threatened to drape it with amendments that would:

Overturn baseball's exemption from the antitrust laws granted by the Supreme Court . . . [in 1922].

Repeal a 1966 law that allowed the two major professional football leagues to merge.

Outlaw local television blackouts when a pro football game is sold out.

The Supreme Court's 1922 ruling that professional baseball was "not a subject of commerce" and was thus exempt from antitrust prosecution was deplored anew . . . [in September 1971] when American League club owners decided to let Robert Short move the Washington franchise.

It wasn't actually the antitrust exemption that allowed Mr. Short to move his franchise, which is his property to locate where he wants within American League rules. Rather than legislating Mr. Short back to Robert F. Kennedy Stadium, congressional repeal of the exemption would represent punishment of baseball for its sins. Or in the words of the angry Representative Sisk, it would administer to the owners the "legal spanking these miscreants are asking for."

The exemption primarily protects organized baseball's "reserve clause" for holding players, its method of drafting rookies and its bargaining with networks for exclusive telecasting of games. It also allows leagues to limit the number of team franchises and to keep interlopers out of the home territories of established teams. . . .

Baseball's antitrust exemption also protects the system by which teams in the two major leagues refrain from competing with each other in offering salaries to rookie players. When a team drafts the right to negotiate with a young player, no other team in either league will try to sign a contract with him for a specified period. Because the National and American League mutually observe this and other rules, they're considered "merged" for all practical purposes.

In contrast to baseball, the courts have held professional football subject to the antitrust laws, which until 1966 prevented football from copying baseball's player draft system. When the National Football League and the American Football League were in actual competition, a young college superstar could choose between escalating bids from a team in each league. The teams complained that the sky-high bidding was driving them into the poorhouse, and in 1966 Congress allowed the leagues to merge. This permitted a more economical one-team, one-rookie contract negotiating system.

Cash, Cadillacs and Mother

Football's common draft now is the envy of the seventeen-team National Basketball Association and the eleven-team American Basketball Association [ABA], which want to merge for the same reasons. "The killing annual competition between the two leagues for untried rookies is the main consideration of our dire financial problems," says Baltimore Bullets owner Abe Pollin in a statement prepared for Senator Ervin's subcommittee. ABA Commissioner Jack Dolph reports that one of his clubs gave a rookie a five-year $900,000 contract, plus a $50,000 bonus, plus a promise of three Cadillacs, and agreed to put his mother on the team public relations payroll. Without a merger, warns a consulting economist for the leagues, as many as ten pro basketball teams could go smash within four years.

Whatever the merits of their case, the basketball owners haven't exactly been lucky so far. Their first setback came as hearings on the merger bill opened last month, when antitrust subcommittee chairman Philip Hart [Democrat] of Michigan decided to let Senator Ervin preside. Senator Hart is sympathetic to the bill. Senator Ervin, in contrast, let the basketball men know right away where they stood. Their bill, he said, "proposes to rob every man in America who possesses skill in basketball of the right to sell his skill to the highest bidder on a free market."

That night in Boston, Robert Short said he was taking the Senators to Texas. When the basketball people re-entered the hearing room the next morning, they found Senator Ervin more hostile than ever. Mr. Short's timing was "very, very damaging," says former California Senator Thomas Kuchel [Republican], legal spokesman for the basketball leagues.

Senator Ervin will keep trying to make basketball owners squirm when hearings resume . . . in [November 1971]. He has asked these "very shrewd and wealthy individuals" to send him personal and corporate financial statements and copies of back tax returns. His written request concluded, deadpan: "Since you are requesting the US Government to allow your team to operate as part of a monopoly in order to permit the growth and success of professional basketball, I assume that you will have no objection to providing this information."

If not much information comes in, as everybody assumes, Senator Ervin will have his excuse to keep the basketball bill hostage. Basketball lawyer Kuchel says the bill preferably should be enacted by late next spring [1972] if the merger is to take place before the 1972-73 season [it did not—Ed.], so the bill's opponents have the tactical advantage of a deadline to stall against. At this point, however, Senator Ervin sounds more interested in bouncing from basketball into a general examination of sports law. "The whole sports system needs investigating," he says. "I don't know of any industries outside football and baseball that are allowed monopolistic power and then allowed to regulate their own monopoly."

That remark might suggest that the Senator wants a Federal regulatory czar for sports, but he insists "I'd hate to have to go that route." His preference is for changes that would require more free enterprise in the sports marketplace, especially when team owners bargain with players and television broadcasters. The same general viewpoint is shared by [former] chairman Emanuel Celler [Democrat, New York] of the House Judiciary Committee.

But 100 percent free enterprise purity in professional sports is impossible, say advocates of antitrust relief. "The problems of the business of sports are quite different from the problems of the marketplace," says Mr. Kuchel. "You've got to apply a different yardstick."

Nebraska's Senator Roman Hruska [Republican], chief sponsor of the basketball bill, thinks it may be necessary to give up "some attributes of free enterprise in return for other benefits like the stability of the game and the increase in the number of player jobs and clubs and one thing and another."

It's the "one thing and another" that bothers Roger Noll, a six-foot, five-inch former college basketball player who specializes in the economics of pro sports at the Brookings Institution . . . [in Washington]. Mr. Noll proposes more selectivity in the special breaks granted sports. "What has to be done," he says, "is to separate out those rules actually necessary to play the game from those that are just used unnecessarily to enrich the owners. All we're saying is that they've gone too far."

The nature of games simply requires some conspiracies. At the start of each season, a fixed number of teams in a league must be allowed to work out a playing schedule, for example. And total free enterprise would allow the New

York Yankees to hire Willie Mays away from the San Francisco Giants in midseason just by offering a bigger salary. That kind of anarchy "is not in the interest of sports," says Mr. Noll.

So a contract should last at least one season to protect the team's roster and to foster fan loyalty. Even that wouldn't be long enough, however, to preserve a team's incentive to operate a farm system in the minors, where a promising young player might toil for several years before his employer feels he's ready for the big leagues.

Curt Flood himself [former star of the St. Louis Cardinals who waged an unsuccessful antitrust suit against the reserve clause before the Supreme Court] has suggested that something like a seven-year contract might be a good compromise between permanent reserve clause slavery and a team's need for time to develop its players to professional maturity. After seven years, the player would be free to shop around for a new employer.

Finally, teams in a given league must continue to conspire on formulas for divvying up gate and TV receipts; Mr. Noll thinks football's 60-40 split of the gate between the home and visiting teams is a strong financial equalizer for the sport, and he wishes baseball and basketball had similarly generous revenue-sharing plans.

Fans and Ticket Prices

But Mr. Noll also lists areas in which he would like to see more competition in the sports business. Besides giving players greater freedom to change teams, the Brookings economist thinks any long-term congressional reform of the sports laws should make it easier for would-be team owners to get new league franchises, even in cities that now are exclusive territorial preserves of existing teams. This would give fans a better choice of games to see, and would put downward pressure on ticket prices. However, it also would bring up the old problem of expansion clubs: A decline in the quality of play as more teams scrape lower for athletic talent.

So what, asks Mr. Noll, as long as the customers come? "The supply of people who can be second-rate athletes is large compared with the number of slots that are open," he says. "There are a lot of people who can play second string in pro sports and populate the rosters."

Even a partial dismantling of the "giant sports trusts" will be difficult, Senator Ervin concedes: "The people who own these clubs wield quite a political clout." But the feeling seems to be growing in Congress that the sports businessmen are abusing their privileges. Senator Tunney is a co-sponsor of the basketball merger bill, and he hopes it passes. But as the bill is considered, he says, "I believe we should expand the investigation to other sports. The public interest has been a subject overlooked—in the movement of franchises, in TV blackouts, in ticket prices—for too long a period."

SPORTS, GAMBLING, AND THE PUBLIC INTEREST [3]

New York City and the state have taken the big gamble on gambling, and at the moment the only thing certain is that nothing is quite what it seems. Mayor John V. Lindsay charged up to Albany this past winter [1970], calling for legalization of off-track betting and estimating that it would net the city $50 million in the first year. But now, with the legislation passed, even City Hall sources admit that $50 million as a starter is optimistic. One of the most powerfully persuasive, two-pronged arguments for legalization was that it would put underworld bookies out of business and end the corruption of the police force. But now, with the law enacted, some bookies are turning handsprings of joy, and law-enforcement officials are almost unanimous in

[3] From "Big Gamble on Gambling: New York's Off-Track Betting," by Fred J. Cook, a free-lance writer, author of *The Secret Rulers*, a study of Mafia activities in New Jersey. *Nation*. 211:9-13. Jl. 6, '70. Reprinted by permission.

the belief that bookmaking will survive—and so will corruption.

This murky situation is far distant from the state of virtuous opulence that New Yorkers have been taught to expect by a twenty-year campaign to legalize off-track betting. The tone was set on January 16, 1950, when the late Mayor William O'Dwyer startled the state legislature by calling for the legalization of gambling. O'Dwyer's brief message contained most of the points that were to be repeated in late April . . . [1970] when the state legislature approved a measure permitting New York City—and other cities of the state above 125,000 in population, if they approved the proposal in local referendums—to set up official off-track horse race betting parlors. O'Dwyer said that law enforcement had been unable to cope with gambling:

> The basic difficulty arises from the widespread human instinct to gamble. . . . To prohibit gambling is simple; to enforce the prohibition, however, raises problems similar to those confronting us in the days of the Prohibition Amendment. Everyone is familiar with the evils surrounding that experiment. . . .
> Instead of permitting a situation to exist where the underworld is able [to] and does obtain tremendous sums in carrying on their activities, the state, through regulation and control, should step in and not only obtain large sources of revenue, but also destroy the underworld's last major source of financial support. . . .

The other side of the debate was stated by [the late] Governor Thomas E. Dewey, who denounced O'Dwyer's suggestions as "shocking, immoral and indecent." He was appalled that government should seek to prey on the weaknesses of its people by dangling "a lure" before their eyes with the establishment of thousands of shops across the state.

The choice lay, as Dewey saw it, between strong and honest law enforcement, with a restricted system of legal on-track betting, and the turning of all America into a replica of Las Vegas. (Even as New York was legalizing off-track betting, the New Jersey legislature was hearing arguments for a proposal to convert Atlantic City into a "Las Vegas of the East.") Dewey argued that our historical experience had demonstrated that "corruption and poverty" had followed gambling wherever it had been legalized. He recalled that, in colonial times and in the early days of the Republic, lotteries had flourished everywhere. Roads and bridges had been built by lottery-raised funds; churches and universities had been financed by them. But the attendant evils had been so great that state after state, not from moral scruples but from tragic sociological experience, had banned gambling in their constitutions. For these reasons, Dewey was "unalterably opposed" to letting down the bars on gambling in New York.

This remained the attitude of Republican-dominated state legislatures and gubernatorial administrations as hard-pressed mayors of New York periodically pleaded for legal gambling to raise revenue. During the two decades of argument and political sparring, the substance of O'Dwyer's proposal changed. O'Dwyer had called for the legalization of betting on sports events of every description, both amateur and professional. Mayor Robert F. Wagner's administration confined itself to arguing for off-track horse race betting. But the Wagner administration, like the Lindsay administration today, still advanced the attractive claim that official betting shops would take the food out of the bookies' mouths and curb official corruption.

This campaign appealed to a broad cross section of New Yorkers. The burden of the city's multibillion-dollar budget was heavy on almost everyone: business and real estate interests, home owners, even commuters hit by the city income tax. With the tax structure threatening to become confiscatory, the prospect of a new and potentially tremendous source of revenue that would be painless to everyone except bookies and the underworld was virtually irresistible. Here, then, in summary, is the way the pro and con argument developed:

The Pro Argument

(1) Gambling is a natural instinct, and the laws against it are just like Prohibition—an effort to legislate private morals that can only result in another blue-nosed disaster. People should be free to do whatever they want, as long as they inflict no positive harm on anyone else. Law enforcement in this view should be confined to two main objectives: the protection of persons and the protection of property.

(2) The underworld is financed by illegal gambling, and its enormous revenue from this source corrupts government on every level. So take all that money away from them, ruin the underworld, and put an end to corruption. Even in O'Dwyer's day the gross illegal betting handle in the New York metropolitan area was estimated at an incredible $5 billion annually; today, national estimates, which some sources call conservative, put the underworld's gross take at some $22 billion a year, with about half of that coming from gambling. Think, say the advocates of legalization, of what we could do for our schools and hard-pressed city governments with all that money.

(3) The present system that makes it legal to bet at the track, but illegal to bet in town is hypocritical and fosters contempt for all law enforcement. This double standard discriminates in favor of the well-to-do against the poorer, working classes. Those who have time and money can go to the track and bet legally; those who can't, but who want to bet on the same horses, must break the law. It's an asinine system, impossible to justify, and must be abolished.

And the Con

(1) Gambling is not an instinct but a cultivated habit; nor does the analogy with Prohibition apply. Liquor is a definite product, one that had been perfectly legal and respectable through all the ages of man until America banned it as a gesture of self-denial during World War I. A person who buys a bottle of liquor or a drink at a bar knows pre-

cisely what he is getting. Drinking, handled sensibly, can serve both health and social purposes. Gambling, on the other hand, is essentially a racket, whether run by the state or the bookie. It is set up so that only the operator can win. (Those millions envisioned by New York mayors do not spring up through cracks in the pavement.) The state clips 16 percent off the top of the parimutuel betting pool on the flat tracks, 17 percent on the harness tracks—and the result is inevitable. The inveterate bettor who keeps bucking that percentage is bound to go broke, and it is both immoral and socially destructive for government to victimize its citizens and so encourage the growth of an emotional gambling fever among its people.

(2) Every step in the legalization process leads to demands for further legalization. If off-track betting is now legal, why shouldn't slot machines and casino gambling be legalized? As Governor Dewey said, there is in logic no place to stop; and the choice lies between a society chasing the rainbow of something-for-nothing and a society in which rewards are based upon work and talent.

(3) Legal off-track betting won't ruin the underworld and end corruption. Horses constitute the lesser part of a bookie's business. Some sources put this play as low as 20 percent. Far larger sums are wagered on both baseball and football, and basketball draws at least as large a play. Even if legal off-track betting took away every dime of the bookies' horse race business—and not even the most optimistic expect that —the bookies would still be doing business at the same old stands, and paying off for the privilege.

(4) The double standard involved in the legal on-track situation isn't as black and white as proponents of legalization claim. A day at the track can be a social affair and a recreational outing, much like going to the theatre or a baseball game. Betting is part of it, but not the whole of it. On the other hand, off-track betting caters to secret vice—to those who have shady money or are dipping their fingers

into the business till; to those who are hooked, but don't want their friends or business acquaintances to know that they are daily plungers, risking hundreds or even thousands of dollars on the outcome of a single ball game or a single race.

Writing in 1965, when off-track betting was again becoming an issue in Albany [*The Nation,* January 18], Milton R. Wessel made the point that "gambling begets more gambling," and predicted that legalization would "prove a tremendous boon to the bookies and the underworld." Mr. Wessel spoke with authority: he had been in charge of a two-year nationwide investigation of organized crime and was chief prosecutor of the 1959 Apalachin "Mafia" trial.

Against this background, it is interesting to trace how the present off-track legalization bill came into being. Mayor Lindsay, faced with an estimated $630 million city deficit, went up to Albany on a quest for additional hundreds of millions of dollars in state aid. "My impression," says one observer who was fairly close to the situation, "is that the mayor initially was not greatly interested in the off-track proposal. It was just something that the city had been calling for ever since 1950, and it was thrown into the package along with a variety of other proposals for consideration in Albany."

Governor Rockefeller and leaders of the legislature were shocked by the size of Lindsay's demand, and especially by his call for another heavy rise in real estate taxes and a five-fold increase in the commuter income tax. The legislators balked at the package as a whole, but it was obvious that the city did require enormous new revenue. To obtain it, the Albany conferees were driven toward the off-track betting proposal which at first they had almost ignored. City voters in a referendum some years earlier had voted overwhelmingly for legalization, so that was a "tax" that legislators could vote for without incurring the wrath of anyone. They could always say they were giving New York City voters just what they wanted.

Nevertheless, after the bill had been passed and signed into law, Governor Rockefeller was obviously ill at ease. In a television interview, he acknowledged that he had always opposed off-track betting; he had been brought up, he said, to believe that gambling was wrong. But then he had re-called that his father, an ardent Prohibitionist, had changed his mind when he saw the harm Prohibition was doing. Per-haps, said the Governor, he was similarly wrong about gambling. Advocates of the bill had argued that it would cripple the mob; if true, that would be a gain. And, finally, the Governor explained, New York City simply had to have additional huge sources of revenue, and there just seemed to be no other way to get it.

The Off-Track Betting Bill

The bill that the legislature passed and the Governor approved did more than legalize off-track betting in cities that approve it by local option; it also revamped the existing state lottery system. The lottery, which has been charging $1 a ticket for monthly drawings, is now authorized to cut the ticket price and hold more frequent drawings. It was proposed that tickets be reduced to as little as 25 cents and sold through vending machines, and that drawings be held on a weekly or semi-weekly basis. This revision is a tacit ad-mission that the lottery has not raised anything approaching the revenue its champions foresaw. It is now hoped that the lower price and more frequent drawings will make it a more effective competitor with the illegal numbers racket. [There is now a weekly state lottery with tickets selling at 50 cents. —Ed.]

While the details remain to be worked out, one gets a fairly clear picture of how New York City's off-track parlors will operate. About one hundred betting shops will be estab-lished in various sections of the city. They must not be lo-cated near churches, schools or unemployment insurance offices. No drinks or beverages can be served; no radio or television accounts of the races given. These are to be "antiseptic" betting parlors, with loitering discouraged after one has placed one's bet. There will be no credit. Bets may be phoned in, but only if the bettor has put up a deposit on which to draw.

Setting up the system will be a formidable job. Not only must the one hundred locations be rented but some five thousand personnel must be hired, and sophisticated electronic equipment installed to funnel the betting play into the local tracks, where the odds will be affected. A special task force named by Mayor Lindsay to speed the process hopes to get the first shop opened by October 1 [1970], by which time much of this year's racing season will be over. However, enthusiasts still talk of reaping something like $200 million a year (which would mean the city would have to handle $1.25 billion a year in bets) when the full system is operating. By which time, they add, the bookies will have left town and official corruption will be a dark memory.

The bookies don't seem to think so. "This is the best thing that ever happened to us," one said. "People are going to bet who never bet before—and a lot of them are going to begin betting with us. I figure it should double my business." Others were less euphoric, but few thought they would be hurt. Their hunch is that customers who bet $500 on a single race will not want Internal Revenue sticking its nose into their business. And besides there are all those other sports. . . . [After a little more than two years of operation, New York's Off-Track Betting can be judged very much a financial success, and there are those willing to argue that it is an ethical success, as well. By the end of 1973, OTB was expected to handle more than $700 million in wagers at its 130 outlets. The system already was featuring computerized telephone accounts with monthly billings, and proposals were being heard for its taking over numbers betting in the city and perhaps off-track betting for the entire state, handling not only wagers on the horses but on a whole range of professional sports from tennis to football. As for bookie operations,

OTB appeared to have won over the great mass of small-time bettors, although the big $1,000 plungers were still said to favor their local confidants.—Ed.]

The Social Issues

Aside from whether the new city system will work, there remain the larger social issues involved in this extension of legalized gambling. Alfred J. Scotti, long-time head of the rackets bureau in the office of District Attorney Frank S. Hogan, sees potential disasters in both the off-track legalization and the extension of the state lottery system. He believes that stolen money or unreported tax money will continue to be played with the bookies; that the need to report winnings from an official betting pool will keep the big plungers away. "And," Scotti adds, "I'm convinced that the system will have a corrosive effect on the whole moral fiber of the community. You will be inducing people to bet, encouraging them to believe they can get something for nothing. The results, I'm afraid, can be disastrous."

Scotti takes an even more pessimistic view of the plan for an expanded state lottery. Unless such a lottery is run on a daily basis, something not now contemplated, it will not put the numbers runners out of business because playing the numbers is a daily addiction. Furthermore, Scotti says:

Morally, this can be worse than off-track betting. . . . Even the school children will be playing the vending machines, out for a quick buck. Everyone will be seeking something for nothing, and it will encourage inertia, discourage using one's energies and abilities to work and do something useful. This could make us so completely money-conscious that it frightens me, and it may convert all of us to the mentality of the criminal. I oppose this even more than off-track betting.

Scotti has expressed these views to a class he teaches at the New School for Social Research. His students, he says, are of above-average intelligence and knowledge—schoolteachers, sociologists, psychologists, policemen, even FBI agents. Both last year and this [1969 and 1970], after he had

finished lecturing on the gambling evil, his class took a vote
on how it felt. "Last year they split 50-50. This year, about
70 percent voted for legalization. I was shocked."

I encountered a similar reaction a couple of months ago
[spring 1970] when I spoke on the subject of organized crime
to a group of liberal-minded, concerned citizens of above-
average intelligence. After I had finished, the questions
came, and it was obvious that the only arguments that had
registered with a good part of my audience were those clichés
about human nature, Prohibition and crippling the underworld that have been used for decades with such great effect
by proponents of legalization.

My experience with this issue goes back to the early 1930s
when, as a cub reporter, I covered one of the first meetings
called to build support for legalizing parimutuel betting in
New Jersey, a prerequisite to reopening the old Monmouth
Park track at Oceanport. There were numbers betting and
horse race betting with the bookies in those days, there was
evidence of police corruption without which such activities
cannot long flourish; and one of the arguments advanced at
the time—which I thought persuasive—was that, if parimutuels were legalized, persons who wanted to bet could
go to the tracks and work off their gambling urges. Along
with the great majority of the New Jersey electorate, I voted
to change the state constitution and permit parimutuel
wagering.

The results, in the record for anyone to read, have been
almost the opposite of what proponents of legalization promised. Next to Prohibition, the greatest boon to the mob in
this century has undoubtedly been the parimutuels. For, as
a number of law-enforcement officials say when discussing
both gambling and narcotics, "addicts create addicts"—and
it makes little difference from the standpoint of spreading
the habit whether the activity is legal or illegal.

The experience in Massachusetts is typical. In 1933 a
crime commission studying conditions in the state did not
even mention gambling and bookmaking as significant

problems. Two years later, like a number of other states desperately seeking additional revenues in the midst of a depression, Massachusetts legalized parimutuels. The result, as another Massachusetts crime commission reported in 1957 after a four-year study, was a wave of large-scale gambling. This later commission dated "the beginning and growth in Massachusetts of the huge business under consideration" from the legalization of parimutuels.

The Perils of Gambling

Virgil W. Peterson, veteran director of the Chicago Crime Commission, years ago published a monograph, *Why Honest People Steal*, his findings being based on a survey of surety companies in every part of the United States. Asked to rate the causes of embezzlement, one of the nation's fastest growing crimes, these companies placed gambling first, followed by extravagant living, unusual family expenses, undesirable associates and inadequate income. "Some companies," Peterson wrote, "estimated that gambling on the part of employees has been responsible for 30 percent of the losses of those companies. Other companies blamed gambling for as high as 75 percent of their total losses."

I can recall at random a large building and loan association that had to be reorganized, a bank that was so looted it failed, and several flourishing businesses that suddenly plunged downhill into bankruptcy—all because some high executives became hooked on horses. Because of such experiences I cannot agree that gambling should be a matter of individual choice; that it hurts no one but the gambler. On the contrary, the record says that it brings with it a cargo of social evils.

This has been proved nowhere more clearly than in Nevada, where gambling has been carried to its logical conclusion. Legalization in Nevada did not drive out the underworld; the underworld took advantage of the opportunity to become legitimate. From the moment when the late Benjamin (Bugsy) Siegel opened his gaudy Flamingo, some of the flashiest Las Vegas casinos have been run by the mob from behind innocent-appearing fronts. As Virgil Peterson wrote:

Legalized gambling has always been attractive to the criminal and racketeering elements. The migration of many of the nation's biggest racketeers to Nevada, where gambling is legal, is the logical and inevitable result of legalization schemes.

Year after year, the Uniform Crime Reports of the FBI put Nevada right up with New York and California in crimes per 100,000 population. Financial crimes—robbery, burglary, larceny—are exceptionally high. In a typical recent year, the Nevada figures showed 2,360.2 crimes per 100,000 to New York's 2,399.6. Its robbery figure was considerably below New York's, but its burglary rate was 931.5 to New York's 940.9, and its larceny rate was 826 to New York's 795.5. Nevada rates are consistently higher than—sometimes more than double—similar rates in the neighboring states of Arizona, Utah and Idaho. The suicide rate in Nevada is usually among the highest in the nation.

Such statistics reinforce Peterson's contention that "from the time of antiquity mass gambling has been a social and economic evil," and that "almost every civilized nation has at one time or another found it necessary to enact prohibitory laws." And they underline the wisdom of Alexis de Tocqueville's observation in *Democracy in America* that governments "must practically teach the community day by day that wealth, fame and power are the rewards of labor, that great success stands at the utmost range of long desires, and that there is nothing lasting but what is obtained by toil."

WHAT WE SPEND ON RECREATION [4]

Over the past two decades spending on leisure in the United States has become recognized as one of the bulwarks

[4] From "The Economics of Recreation Today," by Richard Kraus, a former professor at Teachers College, Columbia University, currently professor in the health and physical education department at Lehman College of the City University of New York. *Parks & Recreation.* 5:19-21+. Je. '70. Reprinted by permission.

of the national economy. In the mid-1960s, the financial columnist, Sylvia Porter, wrote of recreation as "a big booming professional business—dazzling even the most optimistic projections of a few years ago. . . ." More recently, in the January 1970 National Economic Review of the New York *Times,* it was stated:

At the dawning of the seventies, leisure has become an essential part of American life, with a pattern of growth significantly greater than that of the economy. The varied groups in the highly diversified leisure "industry" expect therefore continued expansion of their revenues . . . as the market for their products and services broadens.

While the growth of recreation spending is widely recognized, there is considerable disagreement as to its actual extent in the United States today. Some recent estimates have placed the annual figure at $150-$200 billion. More conservatively, the *Statistical Abstract of the United States,* annually published by the United States Department of Labor, reported in 1969 that the total amount of "personal consumption expenditure for recreation" in the most recent year for which statistics were available, 1967, was $30.6 billion. Obviously, there is a disparity between these estimates.

What is the correct sum? How much do we actually spend on recreation in the United States, and in what ways? First it should be made clear that the *Statistical Abstract of the United States*—authoritative as it may be in other areas—has always underestimated the amount of leisure spending in the United States. For example, in 1959 the *Statistical Abstract* reported consumer expenditure on leisure as $16 billion. Yet in the same year, *Fortune* magazine, a leading financial publication, reported that its economic studies found that the annual sum spent on recreation was $41 billion.

What accounts for this disparity?

In part, the problem is one of defining recreation itself. Should all activities carried on voluntarily within leisure time for pleasure or self-enrichment be regarded as recrea-

*Annual Consumer Spending on Recreation
in the United States in the Late 1960s* *

1.	Books, maps, magazines, newspapers, and sheet music	$ 5.6
2.	Nondurable toys and sports supplies	3.9
3.	Wheel goods, durable toys, sports equipment, pleasure aircraft, and boats	3.4
4.	Radio and television receivers, records and musical instruments	7.4
5.	Radio and television repair	1.2
6.	Camping equipment and supplies	5.0
7.	Swimming pools and accessories	1.0
8.	Equipment and supplies for home "do-it-yourself" activities	12.0
9.	Motion picture houses, gross receipts	1.9
10.	Admissions to legitimate theaters and opera, and entertainment of nonprofit institutions	.6
11.	Spectator sports admissions	.4
12.	Gross receipts, including dues and fees, of clubs and fraternal organizations (luncheon, athletic and social clubs, and school fraternities)	.9
13.	Commercial participant amusements, including billiard parlors; bowling alleys; dancing, riding, skating, shooting, and swimming places; amusement devices and parks, etc.	1.6
14.	Other purchases and fees, including photography, dogs and other pets, collectors' and other hobbies expenses, camping fees, etc.	2.4
15.	Parimutuel betting on thoroughbred and trotting horse racing	5.4
16.	Domestic pleasure travel	32.0
17.	Foreign pleasure travel	5.0
18.	Home entertaining	7.0
19.	Purchase of alcoholic beverages	14.5
20.	Purchase of tobacco and smoking supplies	9.2
21.	Hunting and fishing licenses, equipment and related expenses	4.0
22.	Lawn and garden supplies and equipment	2.0
	Total	**$125.9**

* Stated in billions of dollars.

tion—regardless of their moral desirability or social purpose? If so, spending for such items as liquor (which the *Statistical Abstract* does not include, but which is obviously used recreationally by the bulk of the population) must be included in an analysis of leisure spending. Another problem is the difficulty in determining what portion of a given activity represents recreation. For example, domestic travel in the United States represents a $39 billion industry, not including short local trips. It would appear difficult to determine what portion of this should be regarded as recreation, in the sense of being "vacation" or "pleasure" travel. Yet, economic studies have yielded formulas that make it possible to assign portions of such multipurpose forms of activity to recreation.

Annual Spending on Recreation

Generally, the *Statistical Abstract* has dealt with an extremely narrow range of recreational involvements. A more comprehensive statement of annual spending on recreation in the United States . . . [appears on the preceding page]. It draws on statistics reported chiefly in 1968 and 1969, but to some degree earlier in the 1960s, by the following sources: (a) the Securities Research Division of Merrill, Lynch, Pierce, Fenner and Smith, a leading stockbrokerage firm; (b) *Forbes* magazine, a respected financial publication; (c) the financial section of *U.S. News & World Report;* (d) the annual National Economic Review of the New York *Times;* (e) studies of leisure spending reported by *Life* magazine and *Fortune* magazine; (f) the *Statistical Abstract of the United States*; and (g) various other trade association or industrial reports which have appeared in the press.

It should be made clear that this is a conservative estimate of leisure spending. In a number of cases, the figure cited is clearly a low one. For example:

1. Item 3, taken from the *Statistical Abstract,* includes boating as one of its subitems that add up to a total of $3.4 billion. However, other sources indicate that

pleasure boating alone involved an annual expenditure of $3.1 billion in the late 1960s. Obviously, the total sum should be far higher.

2. Item 14, also taken from the *Statistical Abstract* and including photography as a subitem, adds up to $2.4 billion. However, other economic reports indicate that photography alone involves a total annual expenditure of $3.0 billion.

3. Item 15 reports only the amount of money legally gambled on horse racing. However, authorities have estimated that the total amount of *all* gambling in the United States is $50 billion a year. The Mafia alone is reported to do a $20 billion business annually on illegal betting on sports events and racing.

No attempt has been made to assess spending on narcotics, commercialized vice, or the sale of pornographic materials (books, magazines, pictures, or film). The latter item alone has been estimated to run as high as $2 billion a year in the United States today. Each of these may be regarded as voluntary, pleasure-seeking uses of leisure, although they clearly would not be acceptable forms of community-sponsored recreation activity.

Nor does this report take into account the great number of vacation homes which Americans are building today for clearly recreation purposes. It does not include the recreation facilities being built by apartment or private-home developers, such as community swimming pools, tennis courts, saunas, lounges, clubs, or golf courses, which are generally paid for in rents, the purchase price of homes, or special fees. It does not include the vast amount of commercial spending on recreation development to support such recent ventures as the Astrodome complex in Houston, Texas (over $70 million), the new Madison Square Garden in New York City ($150 million), or the new Disney World . . . in Florida ($160 million). Nor does it include the rapidly increased spending on artistic and cultural activities, except for the figures on admissions to legitimate theaters and opera. It has been calculated that spending on cultural activities alone would comprise a $7 billion expenditure by the early 1970s.

Moreover, this figure does not include other major aspects of recreation expenditures, such as government or voluntary agency programs. These are extremely difficult to calculate, and appear in no economic or professional report or yearbook. However, they may be estimated on the basis of known facts.

Federal Expenditures on Recreation

A major area of Federal spending on recreation is in the provision of outdoor recreation facilities and services. Based on total recorded visitor days in 1968 of the United States Forest Service, the National Park Service, the United States Army Corps of Engineers, the Tennessee Valley Authority, the Bureau of Reclamation and the Bureau of Land Management, and using a cost per visitor-day unit based on the National Park Service operation (an annual budget of $125.5 million to serve 150.8 million visitors), total Federal expenditure on outdoor recreation is estimated at $450 million.

Federal spending on Armed Forces recreation appears in no report or publication. However, it is known that United States Army Special Services employs over 13,000 full-time and 200,000 part-time military and civilian employees, and operates over 1,800 major recreation facilities throughout the world. Similarly, the Air Force, Navy, and Marine Corps operate extensive recreation programs; the total cost of armed forces recreation is estimated here as no less than $300 million. Other Federal costs for recreation, including the provision of therapeutic recreation services in Veterans' Administration and National Institutes of Health Hospitals, support by the Office of Economic Opportunity and the Department of Health, Education, and Welfare of local programs, planning funds and facilities subsidies by Housing and Urban Development and the Model Cities programs, and funds provided by the Land and Water Conservation Act program, would appear to comprise at least $500 million.

Adding all these programs, Federal recreation spending comes to at least $1.25 billion annually.

State and Local Expenditures on Recreation

According to National Conference on State Parks statistics, state park and recreation agencies spent $295 million in 1967. With rapidly accelerating programs of land acquisition and major bond programs for outdoor recreation, conservation, and antipollution efforts in the late 1960s, it would appear that state expenditures for recreation are now in the neighborhood of $400 million per year. Other state recreation programs, including the provision of special services in homes and schools for the retarded, hospitals for the mentally ill, grants to local communities for youth and Golden Age recreation programs, and school-sponsored programs, and the support of professional education in recreation, must add up to at least $100 million per year.

Thus, state spending on recreation is conservatively estimated at $0.5 billion per year.

Spending by local recreation and park agencies rose from $567 million in 1960 to $905 million in 1965. Assuming that this trend has continued, which appears justified by the overall growth of municipal and county facilities and programs, the figure for 1970 is $1.4 billion. This, however, does not include many other forms of recreation programs which are sponsored by departments of welfare, municipal housing agencies, police departments, municipal hospitals, museums, libraries, social service and youth boards, and similar bodies. In New York City, for example, there are at least ten important public departments which offer recreation programs, of which only three are reported in the *Recreation and Park Yearbook*. The total sum spent for local recreation and parks is probably close to $2 billion.

Based on these calculations, all government spending on recreation in the United States is estimated at $3.75 billion per year.

Voluntary Agencies' Expenditures on Recreation

It is equally difficult to estimate spending for recreation by voluntary agencies throughout the United States. There are hundreds of national organizations and thousands of local groups that provide recreation for their membership, or promote recreational activities by offering facilities or leadership to the public at large. No attempt has yet been made to assess the expenditure of religious agencies, nonprofit community centers and settlement houses, youth organizations, agencies serving the ill and disabled, special interest organizations, and similar voluntary groups. However, some statistics are available through annual reports. For example, the Boy Scouts of America had a national operating budget of $8.6 million and spent $60.3 million through local councils in 1967. The annual operating budget of the Boys' Clubs of America in the same year was $28.9 million. The Young Men's Christian Association had an income of about $234 million in 1968, of which a sizable portion must have been spent to support athletic, cultural, and social programs. Considering the number and diversity of similar organizations throughout the United States, it seems reasonable to assume that they spend at least a billion dollars a year on recreation activities and facilities.

Finally, it was reported in the late 1960s that American industries and business concerns were spending $1.5 billion a year for employee recreation programs and services.

Putting all these figures together, one arrives at the total of $132.15 billion being spent each year for recreation in the United States today. This figure is supported by comparison with a regional study reported by the Southern California Research Council in 1968, which found that in the Southern California region, serving a total population of 12.3 million persons, $9.89 billion was spent annually on recreation. Extrapolating this to the total population of the United States (slightly over 200 million persons in the late 1960s) would mean the nation as a whole spent about $160 billion a year for recreation. However, since the Southern California climate is generally more favorable for recreation and the population more affluent (although it includes sizable numbers of retired older persons on small incomes), it would seem reasonable to reduce the overall figure by approximately 15 percent. This would yield a national figure of $137 billion—extremely close to the total of $132 billion arrived at earlier.

This sum can be appreciated by comparing it to the national expenditure on all forms of education, public and private, which consisted of $58.5 billion in 1968. What do these statistics mean? First, they reflect growth of the national economy during the 1960s. In this period, the Gross National Product rose from $589 billion in 1963 to $861 billion in 1968 and, despite the effects of inflation, the spendable per capita income of the average American rose by one third. The growing use of discretionary income to satisfy leisure interests demonstrates the increased value placed on recreation in modern society. Yet, it also illustrates that Americans are accustomed to spending much greater sums privately for recreation than they are to supporting essential public programs and services. The imbalance between private spending on recreation ($125.9 billion) and public, voluntary-agency or employee-program spending ($6.25 billion) has meant that many recreation and park operations serving the public at large have been starved for financial support.

Cities Caught in Financial Squeeze

A number of the larger cities of the nation have been caught in a traumatic financial squeeze by declining tax bases and the need to provide ever more costly welfare, educational, law-enforcement, housing, transportation, and environmental services. In such cities, recreation and parks have been placed in a precarious position on the budgetary totem pole. As a single example, in New York City during the spring of 1969, budget cuts were announced that slashed recreation and park and school-sponsored programs by several millions of dollars. Important summer and year-round activities were eliminated, hiring "freezes" placed into effect, and museums, libraries, and botanical gardens compelled to reduce their visiting hours or to impose new visitor fees.

On the Federal level, there has been a comparable lack of adequate financial support. The Land and Water Conservation Fund has not had, since its inception in 1965, the amount of money for recreation resource development envisioned in the original legislation. The National Park Service was compelled by the Revenue and Expenditure Control Act of June 1968 to carry out a drastic personnel rollback which resulted in sharply curtailing park and recreation area seasons and operations. In the light of a recent economic study which showed that travel to the National Parks generates $6.4 billion in overall expenditures each year, contributing $5.7 billion to the Gross National Product and $4.7 billion in personal income, this kind of short-sighted economy is sheer idiocy.

In a number of other areas the Federal Government has been equally penurious. Each year, Congress has provided funds for the National Endowment for the Arts, to assist cultural programs throughout the nation, that are actually less than the money provided by some European cities to support municipal opera companies or symphony orchestras. Today, with a number of major American symphony orchestras in danger of imminent bankruptcy because of rapidly rising costs, the need for increased Government subsidy is crucial. As another example, the total budget of the President's Council on Physical Fitness and Sport in 1969 was only $317,000—a ridiculously small sum compared to the amounts spent by other nations to promote fitness and sport. In February 1970, it was announced that the Office of Economic Opportunity would no longer fund special community recreation programs although it had, over the past several years, provided substantial sums for recreation and cultural activities in disadvantaged urban neighborhoods.

Generally, park and recreation administrators have responded to such financial strictures by moving in the direction of "pay-as-you-go" resource and program development. More and more new facilities are being developed in municipal and county programs with the expectation that their costs will be substantially met by fees and charges. If all citizens could afford to pay the generally reasonable fees attached to such facilities or programs, this might be a logical solution for the problem.

However, even within today's affluent society, it has been estimated that 25.4 million persons have family incomes below the minimum subsistence level. Such families, living at the bare edge of necessity, with less than $3,500 or $3,600 for an urban family of four, cannot possibly afford to use the kinds of commercial recreation opportunities cited earlier in this article. They are largely dependent on the network of recreation and park facilities and programs provided by public agencies for constructive leisure opportunities. To permit such programs to depend increasingly upon fees and charges to support capital development and current operations will mean, more and more, that poor people will be excluded from all but the most minimal and barren facilities.

The President's Advisory Commission on Civil Disorder documented the necessity of providing adequate recreation and park facilities in our cities. If this is to be done, without excluding the economically disadvantaged, it will be necessary for us to rethink our priorities as a nation to insure that a fuller portion of the huge sums which today are spent on recreation are used to support vitally needed public and voluntary programs and facilities.

While we may be impressed by the fact that Americans today spend over $132 billion each year to meet leisure needs, this does not mean very much in impoverished neighborhoods in our cities and towns, where the only recreation opportunities are likely to be limited to a poorly equipped, littered, and unattended playground—or to the corner bar. Our public and private expenditures on recreation need to be placed more nearly in balance.

BIBLIOGRAPHY

An asterisk (*) preceding a reference indicates that the article or a part of it has been reprinted in this book.

BOOKS AND PAMPHLETS

*Alden, John. Winning the off-track bet. Doubleday. '73.

Amdur, Neil. The fifth down. Coward. '71.

Arlott, John and Daley, Arthur. Pageantry of sport, from the age of chivalry to the age of Victoria. Hawthorn. '68.

*Barry, Rick. Confessions of a basketball gypsy: the Rick Barry story. Prentice-Hall. '72.

Beisser, A. R. The madness in sports. Appleton. '67.

Boyle, R. H. Sport—mirror of American life. Little. '63.

Brasch, Rudolph. How did sports begin? McKay. '70.

Brasher, Christopher, ed. The road to Rome. Kimber. '60.

Burton, Bill, comp. Sportsman's encyclopedia. Grosset. '71.

Debevec, R. M. Law and the sportsman. Oceana. '59.

Durso, Joseph. All-American dollar: the big business of sports. Houghton. '71.

Edwards, Harry. The revolt of the black athlete. Free Press. '69.

Farr, Finis. Black champion. Scribner. '64.

Gallico, P. W. Farewell to sport. Books for Libraries. '70.

Goodhart, Philip and Chataway, Christopher. War without weapons. W. H. Allen. '68.

Grieve, Andrew. Legal aspects of athletics. A. S. Barnes. '69.

*Hoch, Paul. Rip off the big game. Doubleday. '72.

Izenberg, Jerry. How many miles to Camelot? The All-American sport myth. Holt. '72.
Review. New York *Times Book Review.* p 41. O. 15, '72.

Johnson, Jack. Jack Johnson is a dandy. New American Library. '70.

Johnson, W. O. Jr. All that glitters is not gold; the Olympic game. Putnam. '72.

Lawther, John. Sport psychology. Prentice-Hall. '72.

Loy, J. W. and Kenyon, G. S. eds. Sport, culture and society. Collier. '69.

215

Lucas, Bob. Black gladiator. Dell. '70.
Meggyesy, David. Out of their league. Ramparts. '71.
    Excerpts with title: Football racket. *Look*. 34:66+. N. 17; 64-6+. D. 1, '70.
Mitchell, Brian, ed. Today's athlete. Pelham Books. '70.
Oliver, Chip. High for the game. Morrow. '71.
Olsen, Jack. The black athlete; a shameful story. Time-Life Books. '68.
*Parrish, Bernie. They call it a game. Dial. '71; paper ed. New American Library.
    Review. Time. 98:63. S. 13, '71.
Peterson, R. W. Only the ball was white. Prentice-Hall. '70.
Rudolph, Frederick. The American college and university. Knopf. '62; paper ed. Random House.
Russell, Bill. Go up for glory. Coward. '66.
Sage, G. H. ed. Sport and American society. Addison-Wesley. '70.
Scott, Jack. The athletic revolution. Free Press. '71.
Shecter, Leonard. The jocks. Paperback Library. '70.
Singer, Robert. Coaching, athletics, and psychology. McGraw. '72.
Tunis, J. R. $port$: heroics and hysterics. Day. '28.
Veeck, Bill. The hustler's handbook. Putnam. '65.
Weiss, Paul. Sport: a philosophic inquiry. Southern Illinois University Press. '71.

PERIODICALS

America. 124:321. Mr. 27, '71. New enemy; Ali-Frazier fight and business profits. S. J. Adamo.
American Economist. 13:6-30. Fall '69. Collusive competition in major league baseball: its theory and institutional development. D. S. Davenport.
Annals of the American Academy of Political and Social Science. 389:63-70. My. '70. Outdoor recreation economics. J. V. Krutilla and J. L. Knetsch.
*Atlantic. 227:62-8. Ap. '71. Orr effect. Tom Dowling.
Business Week. p 109-10. Je. 1, '68. Personal business: liability for sports accidents.
Business Week. p 97-8. Ag. 3, '68. Personal business: luxury homes beside the fairway.
Business Week. p 56-8. Ja. 10, '70. The pro in football stands for profits.
Business Week. p 74+. F. 28, '70. Players go to bat against baseball [challenge to professional baseball's "reserve system," the complex set of rules by which club owners can hold, trade, sell, or fire their players as they see fit].

*Business Week. p 77-8. Mr. 6, '71. Country clubs fall short of the green: private golf clubs suffer a financial squeeze as the recession slices income.

*Business Week. p 38-9. Ag. 28, '71. College sports feel budget ax: even football is being dropped as hard-pressed schools try to save their athletic programs.

Business Week. p 60-1+. O. 9, '71. Antitrusters take on professional sports; pursuit of profits prompts Congress to ask: what's the real name of the game?

Canadian Journal of Agricultural Economics. 19:72-85. O. '71. Economic evaluation of big game hunting: an Alberta case study. W. S. Pattison and W. E. Phillips.

*Christian Science Monitor. 65:1. F. 26, '73. On bubblegum and baseball. Ross Atkin.

Dun's. 95:44-7. Ap. '70. Great golf tournament; corporate action. R. Levy.

Ebony. 26:143-7+. N. '70. Annual football roundup; the year of the strike.

Ebony. 27:99-100+. F. '72. Take the money and run! black collegiate basketball stars strike it rich in pro basketball. L. J. Banks.

*Ebony. 27:152-4+. Je. '72. How much is a player worth?

*Economist. 236:50-1. Jl. 11, '70. The £2 billion golf business.

*Editorial Research Reports. v 2, no 9:679-86. S. 1. '71. Professional athlete. R. L. Worsnop.

*Forbes. 107:24-6+. Ap. 1, '71. Who says baseball is like ballet?

Harper's Magazine. 245:40+. N. '72. Giant in the tube: football nation's number one sport. Anton Myrer.

Industrial Development. 139:18-20. Mr./Ap. '70. Golf courses: a profitable component of the resort complex. R. M. Spray.

Journal of Property Management. 36:176-9. Jl./Ag. '71. Profits on the green [the economics of golf course development and management]. C. E. Robinson.

Look. 34:68-72+. O. 20, '70. Green and leafy football; small college answer to big time madness. Stan Isaacs.

Media-Scope. 13:46-8+ N; 42-5+. D. '69; 14:42-4+. Ja. '70. Sell it with sports—the universal language; the cluttered world of sports and media; sports publications—the rush is on. Frank Reysen.

*Nation. 211:9-13. Jl. 6, '70. Big gamble on gambling; New York's off-track betting. F. J. Cook.

*Nation's Business. 59:70-2. D. '71. Winning is a many splendored thing.

*New Statesman. 84:968-70. D. 29, '72. The moneybags of British sport. Clifford Makins.

New Times (Moscow). p 28-31. Jl. 15, '70. Sport, business and
   politics [business sponsorship of various kinds, managerial
   pressures and political patronage]. A. Grigoryev.
*New York Times. p 14S. D. 31, '72. Americans spent more money
   and more time just playing.
*New York Times. p 1+. Ja. 14, '73. Business in a front seat for
   today's super bowl. Tom Buckley.
Newsweek. 71:62. Je. 24, '68. Odd couples; Roosevelt raceway's
   computer dating project to interest youth.
Newsweek. 75:63-4. Ap. 6, '70. Million-dollar war.
Newsweek. 75:58. My. 4, '70. Las Vegas on the Hudson? legalizing
   off-track betting.
Newsweek. 75:68. Je. 8, '70. No-strike season; new contract.
*Newsweek. 76:82. Jl. 13, '70. Promotion: selling the Senators.
Newsweek. 77:94-5. Mr. 8, '71. Take the money and run; Muham-
   mad Ali-Joe Frazier fight promoters.
*Newsweek. 77:75D-76. Mr. 22, '71. Greed creed: will it pay off?
   [closed-circuit TV in sports]
Parks & Recreation. 5:25. Ja. '70. It's big business!
*Parks & Recreation. 5:19-21+. Je. '70. The economics of recrea-
   tion today. Richard Kraus.
*Reader's Digest. 100:146-9. Mr. '72. In pro sports, the dollar is
   king. Bill Surface.
Saturday Review. 54:10-11. Jl. 3, '71. Trade winds: efforts to block
   closed-circuit bullfight in Madison Square Garden. Cleveland
   Amory.
Saturday Review. 54:65-7+. O. 9, '71. Sportswriting, and the All-
   American dollar. Joseph Durso.
Scottish Journal of Political Economy. 18:121-46. Je. '71. The eco-
   nomics of professional football [soccer]: the football club as
   a utility maximiser. P. J. Sloane.
Senior Scholastic. 98:17. My. 3, '71. New line-up for baseball. H. L.
   Masin.
Social Science Quarterly. 52:248-60. S. '71. The economics of "big-
   time" intercollegiate athletics. J. V. Koch.
Sports Illustrated. 28:75-6+. My. 13, '68. Some who know the
   score. Joe Jares.
Sports Illustrated. 30:18-21. Ap. 7, '69. Curse of the endless playoff;
   affliction of pro hockey, basketball, and baseball, now spreading to pro football. Tex Maule.
Sports Illustrated. 32:40+. F. 2, '70. Buy a basketball franchise and
   join the war; pro basketball as big business. Frank Deford.

Sports Illustrated. 32:18-20+. Je. 1, '70. This saint has been called a sinner; Ernie Wheelwright, owner of New Orleans bar with Mafia connections. Morton Sharnik.

Sports Illustrated. 33:40-1. Ag. 24, '70. Hula, moolah and no blahs, the Hawaiian Islanders. R. F. Jones.

Sports Illustrated. 33:78+. S. 21, '70. He cried all the way to the bank; eleventh game, USC vs Alabama. P. F. Putnam.

Sports Illustrated. 33:18-22. N. 16, '70. What a way to make a living; pro football.

Sports Illustrated. 34:10-15. Ja. 4, '71. Rushing to stake a claim; Super bowl gold. Tex Maule.

Sports Illustrated. 34:18-20+. F. 1, '71. Grim run to fiscal daylight; college football in financial squeeze. Patricia Ryan.

Sports Illustrated. 34:56-8+. Ap. 19, '71. But it looked like a great new racket: pro tennis; ed. by Frank Deford. Bob Briner.

Sports Illustrated. 35:36-40+. O. 18, '71. Hockey is here with dollars up and fists down. Mark Mulvoy.

Sports Illustrated. 35:22-3. D. 13, '71. $40 million body shuffle; player trading by big league managers. William Leggett.

Sports Illustrated. 36:40-2+. My. 29, '72. Look what Louie wrought; Emprise and involvement of organized crime in sport. John Underwood and Morton Sharnik.

Sports Illustrated. 36:74-82+. Je. 19, '72. Biggest cheapskate in big D: Lamar Hunt. Jack Olsen.

Sports Illustrated. 37:16-18+. Jl. 24, '72. Would you buy a used playbook from this man? Karl Sweetan's attempted sale of L.A. Rams' book. Tex Maule.

*Sports Illustrated. 37:56-8+. O. 2, '72. There is a disease in sports now. Tom Meschery.

Sports Illustrated. 37:54-6+. O. 9, '72. Charlie O. eyes a pennant or three. Ron Fimrite.

Sports Illustrated. 37:62-3. O. 9, '72. Money makes the puck go. Mark Mulvoy.

Sunset. 145:36. D. '70. Golden Eagle returns for 1971; national recreation fee system.

Time. 96:53. N. 16, '70. Hustling the Heisman hopefuls.

*Time. 97:88-9+. My. 24, '71. Jeremiah of Jock liberation.

*U.S. News & World Report. 67:82-4. S. 22, '69. Pro football's boom; from sport to glamour industry.

U.S. News & World Report. 68:74-5. My. 4, '70. Instead of tax hikes, horse parlors.

*U.S. News & World Report. 71:56-8. Jl. 5, '71. Pro sports: a business boom in trouble.

*U.S. News & World Report. 72:60-1. F. 14, '72. Does it pay to be host to Olympics?

*Vogue. 157:186-7+. My. '71. Men behind the men who make money in sports. Pete Axthelm.

*Wall Street Journal. p 1+. S. 9, '69. The front office: owning a sports team looks like fun, but it isn't always gold mine—many clubs are in red; some owners play down profit, but inefficiency is factor. F. C. Klein.

*Wall Street Journal. p 1+. O. 8, '70. Playing the game: sports-crazy colleges continue to lure stars with improper offers. David DuPree.

Wall Street Journal. p 1+. Mr. 3, '71. Going for broke: promoting a big fight may not be bonanza that it first seemed—Ali-Frazier bout surrounded by money, but who gets how much money is the question. Les Gapay.

*Wall Street Journal. p 20. O. 20, '71. Blowing the whistle on pro sports. A. J. Large.